THE TAO
ℭℨ OF ℬ
STORYTELLING

30 WAYS TO CREATE EMPOWERING STORIES TO LIVE BY

Foreword by Nick Williams

CLAIRE TAYLOR

Balloonview

Copyright © Claire Taylor 2013

A CIP catalogue record for this book is available from the British Library.

ISBN 978-1-907798-31-3

The right of Claire Taylor to be identified as the author of this work has been asserted by her in accordance with the Copyright Designs and Patent Act 1988.

Kind acknowledgement is made to Cló Iar-Chonnacht, Indreabhán, Co. na Gaillimhe, Ireland for permission to reprint 'Subh Milis' by Seamus O' Neill from his book Dhanta do Phasti, first published in 1949.

Photograph by: Simon Martin, Brackley, Northamptonshire.

Printed and bound in Great Britain by
CPI Group (UK) Ltd, Croydon, CR0 4YY

Dedicated to my mother, Della, and my grandmother, Catherine, who are always with us – because they live with the Angels.

CONTENTS

A STORY OF GRATITUDE

Everything we do is made possible because of other people who give us their time, wisdom and love. And so it was with writing *The Tao of Storytelling*. I'm on the planet, writing a book, because of my parents. So, firstly, to Mum and Dad – thank you for having me.

Growing up in Ireland, I was the second eldest of five children. My sister Mary was eighteen months old when I arrived on the scene. Nineteen months later our first brother was born. To my grandmother's delight, my parents called him William in honour of my grandfather's memory but now we call him Bill. For several years, there were just three of us siblings. Then, one day, my parents went out together and Dad returned alone – to tell us that our Mum would be back in a few days' time with our new baby sister. We were excited by the idea of a new baby – like a doll that we could play with. Edel arrived home with our Mum shortly after that. And then we were four!

That is, until much later, when I was thirteen and my parents, who had already decided that we were complete as a family (well, that's Dad's story), discovered that the Universe had a different idea by surprising them with our youngest brother, whom they called Tom after my father.

And so I grew up with my four siblings, my parents and my grandmother (my Mum's mother), who lived with us for several years. With these seven, I have lived through hundreds and probably thousands of stories. A handful of these shared stories have reached this book, together with several others from other times in my life. I'm grateful to my family for the rich history of stories that we shared together in childhood and which we continue to share together as adults, albeit less frequently.

Each of my four siblings has read several of the stories in draft form and given their perspectives on those times we shared together. Mary and Edel kindly reviewed the stories and the exercises in the book.

When I was wondering what to call my book, Edel came up with a great idea for the title – *The Tao of Storytelling*. It's perfect as it encapsulates the magic that happens between the storyteller and the audience of listeners or readers.

Several of my aunties and my uncle also pop up in the stories and I'm grateful to them too – you'll meet them as you read the book.

For many years I wanted to write a book, but it wasn't the right time. Then, one day in July 2011, the time *was* right and I was ready to begin my storytelling journey. I'm grateful to Nick Williams who inspired me to start writing again. Nick is the author of several books, including *The Work We Were Born to Do*, and he is co-founder of Inspired Entrepreneur. He has been a great mentor and friend for over a decade and has written the foreword to this book.

When I began writing *The Tao of Storytelling* I didn't know the steps I needed to take to turn my writing into a book and get it out into the world. Fortunately, there are some wonderful people who do, to whom I'm incredibly grateful. Ed Peppitt from Balloon View metaphorically held my hand on the journey to hatching my fledgling book. Sue Lascelles is a gifted editor to whom I'm eternally grateful for polishing my precious manuscript, while gracefully retaining its essence. Editor Wanda Whitely reviewed an early draft manuscript several months before publication and gave me some excellent and practical wisdom to help me get the manuscript into shape. Beverley Glick is an editor and story archeologist who helped me convey the essence of the book in just a few words on the back cover. With her incredible eye for detail, Caroline Swain has proof read the text for me, making sure that it's grammatically perfect – leaving no i without its dot or t without its cross!

Back in 2012, I spent five weeks at the International School of Storytelling in Sussex. I'm especially thankful to my storytelling mentors on the course, Sue Hollingsworth and Ashley Ramsden – co-founders of the school. I'm also grateful to have met and made friends with several other budding storytellers who were on the same course as me.

I'm blessed to have the support of wonderful friends in my mission to get this book into the world. From the day I began the story blog I was spurred on by the encouragement they have given me. I'm especially thankful to the trainers and friends from Psychology of Vision, UK and International, and to the supportive Inspired Entrepreneur Community.

I'm immensely grateful to my clients and business colleagues too and especially to those who have courageously courted innovative approaches to marketing and leadership. It is only with the engagement of people who are curious, open and brave that new ideas get the opportunity to bloom.

Creating a book has an outer element and an inner element; and so I'm ever grateful to the four wonderful women who have supported me on a spiritual level as I've been birthing my book. Catherine Ward, who is an amazing Energy Healer, told me a few years ago that this book was waiting to be born and has supported me on my journey; Linda Barlow who is a Psychotherapist taught me how to do Transcendental Meditation which has helped me to relax and calm my buzzing mind; and Sarah Alexander, a Spiritual Intelligence Coach, who has helped me to become more connected with my intuition. Sister Eileen Rafferty is a Spiritual Director who, I'm proud to say, is also my Auntie. Since the moment I began the blog of stories that preceded this book, she has given me immense encouragement to keep writing.

On a daily basis for eighteen years now, my darling husband, David, and I have been creating wonderful life stories since our twenties – and his love and support while I've been writing this book have been, and always are, precious. I'm so grateful also for his design talent and his technological genius, which help me to flourish in the modern electronic world. Ryan, my son, has and continues to be one of the greatest catalysts for me to love, learn and grow in my life and I feel blessed to be his Mum. And, finally, thanks to Sage, our gorgeous dog who fills our lives with enthusiastic bounciness.

With love and gratitude to you all!

FOREWORD

by Nick Williams

When I first came across the idea that the Universe is made of stories rather than atoms, something awoke within me. Stories and myths are powerful: they are a fundamental instrument of thought. We live in a world made of more story than stuff. We all tell stories, whether we realise it or not, and our lives are woven from the stories we tell. We tell stories about ourselves to ourselves; we tell stories about ourselves to each other; we tell stories about each other. The stories we buy in to and tell are really the greatest determining factor in the quality of our lives. I am sure that part of the boom in coaching and counselling really has its roots in our search to feel validated and to be able to identify what story it is that we are telling the world about ourselves. We wish to tell more inspiring stories about who we are and why we are here. We want to be proud of being human.

However, we live in a world in which traditional myths are disappearing. The stories told to us by the Church and government no longer have the power over us that they once did. At the same time, we hunger to hear great stories told well, which is why many of the highest paid people on the planet today are storytellers. So whenever a writer, a filmmaker, a corporate brand or a spiritual teacher tells us an inspiring story, we are intrigued and want to sign up to their creation. The hunger we feel for meaning in our life is fed.

Claire is passionate about story. During the twelve years I have known Claire, she has been on a mission to combine her incredible corporate branding and leadership skills with her passion for creativity and storytelling and to bring them into a unified whole. Claire is passionate about stimulating authentic dialogue both inside organisations and between organisations and their customers and partners. The result of these deeper more authentic interactions, she knows, is greater business success, because of the resonance they generate. Her co-founding of the Story Mill together with her husband, David, and her writing of this book are the public manifestations of her quest.

One of the most wonderful aspects of storytelling is that the more authentically personal we become in telling our own story, the more we touch upon something universal. As we share our experience of life, other people say or think, 'Me too.' We all feel validated and reassured. We recognise our shared humanity. By sharing her own stories so honestly, Claire touches the hearts and minds in all of us. She tells stories that remind us of our greatness of spirit, our heroic nature, and which validate and affirm the essential goodness within us. At the same time, she validates and encourages our acceptance of our humanness, our vulnerabilities and our fears. Claire's invitation is for us all to become more honest, open and authentic in the conversations we have and the stories we tell.

By being totally authentic in our humanness – our human frailties as well as our strengths, our self-perceived short-comings as well as our triumphs, our darkest hours as well as our shining moments – we set the stage for becoming the shining examples of triumph over adversity that we truly are, with grace. Claire wants organisations to be places where all aspects of the human spirit are welcomed. Thank you, Claire, for the work you are doing and the trail you are blazing.

Nick Williams,
London, August 2013

IN THE BEGINNING

T*he Tao of Storytelling* is a wisdom memoir with serendipitous roots. What began as an inspired exercise in reclaiming the sense of enchantment that I knew as a child has taken me on an incredible two-year journey into exploring the power of stories. It has led to my co-founding of The Story Mill, an organisation that encourages the use of story as an innovative tool in organisations.

I believe that the stories we tell and buy into are the stories that we live by. These can be about people, places or things. They can be stories that we have told ourselves about: ourselves, our neighbours, our friends or people that we work with. They can be stories that we believe about products, services and especially brands, that are offered to us in our everyday lives.

Stories are a form of conversation and conversations make the world go around. We spend most of our waking hours in the exchange of ideas, thoughts and activities with other people; and much of this exchange is done through the use of anecdotes. Businesses are no different. They comprise real people having conversations through which to exchange ideas, collaborate on goals, negotiate for resources, tell customers about their brands and achieve a myriad of other things.

There was a time when the world was more localised and businesses were smaller. There was greater scope for real conversations to take place. People would visit the corner shop, for example, and interact with the owner, talking about everything from the weather to family, to where the eggs were sourced. Conversations were more raw and honest.

Yet the world has become obsessed with processing everything and our conversations have followed suit – especially in business, which has left a dearth of real heartfelt communication. We know that over processed food is not the most nourishing for our bodies; similarly, engineered communication does not nourish our souls. While our minds might buy the superficial spiel for a while, our hearts, our souls and our spirits know the difference, and we find ourselves longing for something that is richer and more authentic.

So how do we marry the need to communicate widely, with touching people on a deeper personal level in ways that manufactured communication doesn't achieve? It is through the means that humans have used to pass on wisdom for aeons: by telling stories. Stories have the power to communicate broadly, be memorable and easy to share. Why? Because great stories both resonate universally and touch us deeply on a personal level. That is why myths and legends have been used through the ages to communicate universal themes.

Storytelling is not the reserve of a few talented individuals who have kissed the Blarney Stone in Ireland and received its mythological gift of fluent chatter. The stories that we tell, or even subconsciously believe about ourselves, affect the way we live our lives. Our stories are influenced by what other people, especially those whom we regard as authority figures, have said to us in the past and say to us now. We are continuously taking in new information that makes us rethink and evolve our perspectives, which means that we are creating internal dialogues and revising our stories all the time.

Most of us have bought into other people's stories about us and about the way the world is. Indeed, advertisers know and leverage our penchant for a great story. While buying into other people's stories can be helpful if they are empowering, we can often find ourselves unwittingly living by them even when they are not.

Once we become aware of the stories that we have subconsciously been telling ourselves in the past, we have the power to choose which ones we want to live by in the future. We can see how our old tales continue to affect our lives today – even if, as is often the case, they are rooted in our childhoods.

The great contradiction inherent in personal stories is that from the perspective of each teller their story is true. Therefore, two people who have experienced the same set of circumstances might tell very different stories about it, each believing that their version is true. To them, it is.

So how do we create our stories and, more importantly, why do we become attached to believing in them? Well, it is human nature to attempt to make sense of the circumstances of our own and other peoples' lives. Our stories are created through our internal dialogue, which is influenced in turn by the decisions we have made about the world around us. Our stories tell us a great deal about the meanings that we attach to certain events and information. They are a window into our soul, revealing our deeply held values and beliefs and often who we believe we are and our purpose in the world. We grow attached to them because they resonate at deep levels within our psyche. So while we're constantly revising some of our tales, others might need a lot of soul searching to change – before we can do so, we might need to transform some of our self-concepts and the opinions that we have held about others or about the nature of the world.

Our ability to choose the stories we tell about our circumstances is beautifully illustrated by Viktor Frankl in his book *Man's Search for Meaning*, in which he describes his years as a concentration camp inmate. He remarks on the generosity of some prisoners despite the their plight: 'Everything can be taken from a man but one thing: the last of the human freedoms – to choose one's attitude in any given set of circumstances, to choose one's own way.'

The resonance that we experience when we hear a story is because, at their heart, powerful stories have themes that ring universally true, such as 'trust and betrayal', 'good and bad', 'winner and loser', 'victim and perpetrator', 'shame and pride', 'life and death'. They often contain the sorts of archetypal characters that the Swiss psychiatrist and psychologist Carl Jung referred to in his work and which we can all recognise, such as the Innocent, the Warrior, the King, the Hero, the Jester. We can all relate to the energies that are embodied in these characters.

Our individual stories will be steeped in our culture and environment and influenced by these, but the meanings and universal truths within them transcend culture, environment and time. That is why many of the ancient myths and legends have survived for hundreds, even thousands of years, and their underlying meanings still resonate with us today. In my stories, especially the childhood ones, you'll notice that I talk about the backdrop of beliefs that came from growing up in an Irish Catholic family and the celebrations we had around Christmas. However, I'm not religious and this book is not affiliated with any particular religion or creed. You'll see that in the later stories I talk more generally about a Higher Consciousness and the Universe, because I personally believe that there is a universal power that is greater than each of us humans.

That brings me to the *Tao of Storytelling*. The Tao is an Eastern philosophical concept that signifies the essence or nature of the Universe: it is a quality that cannot be described in words or named. As soon as we name something, it becomes a thing – and the Tao is 'no thing': it is an intangible essence. Great stories also have an essence and the experience of hearing a powerful anecdote is indescribable. A story contains, of course, the words, the plot and the characters – but a story is much more than that. It is what you hold in your heart, your mind and even your soul when a story truly resonates with you. It is because of the Tao or essence of storytelling that we prefer stories that are authentic versus those that are manufactured with the aim of seducing us into changing our behaviour.

Authentic stories emerge from a heartfelt place.

We all have a rich repertoire of life stories, many of which might be serving us well while others might be our Achilles' heel. It's easy to think that our stories are not relevant because they were not wild or traumatic, but, while many of us carry with us tales related to seemingly trivial things, those narrative constructs may be supporting negative self-concepts that affect our ability to succeed in particular areas of our lives today. These anecdotes could be about our abilities or talents or money, or what we believe we deserve in life, or about happiness or love or work or relaxation, or a myriad of other things.

Since we all have our own personal stories, when we get together with other people in a working environment, or indeed in any relationship, we carry all the baggage of these with us; and that's when both the fun and the trouble begin.

When we have emotional energy tied up in our stories, and particularly when this energy is negative, there is the potential to create conflict.

The place to begin exploring stories lies within ourselves. Having done this myself, I can promise you that it is incredibly rewarding. You will be surprised and delighted by the experience. If you courageously explore the darker stories in your life, as well as the light ones, you will discover your richest treasure, because underneath our more challenging stories often lie our greatest gifts.

As you read the book, you will find exercises designed to help you discover the treasures from your own stories. I encourage you do that – it is an exciting, insightful and rewarding adventure and I applaud your commitment to your own journey. One caveat, if you have experienced abuse and trauma in your life, please seek advice and support from a professional who is qualified in counselling to help you address those traumatic events from your past. In contrast, the exercises in *The Tao of Storytelling* are coaching based in nature and are not a substitute for professional medical advice or counselling. They are designed to help you to reflect gently on the stories you have created about your world and see how you can create new and more empowering narratives by which to live.

Life lessons are not linear: we learn when the time is right for us to do so and, similarly, the lessons in the book do not necessarily build upon each other, although they *do* follow the chronological order in which life brought them to me – from childhood to the present day. They can be approached on an individual basis, but I think you will find it easiest to follow the thread of the stories if you read the book from beginning to end. Then you can dip into it, selecting a story at random as your thought for the day or the week.

The journey begins here – I hope that you enjoy it!

1. STUMBLING UPON TREASURE

I
t all began on a bright Sunday in June 2011 as I sat in a London workshop run by Nick Williams, discovering the work I was born to do. In April, at the start of the programme, I was sure I knew what my vocation was. But by July I was yearning for a greater sense of heart and soul connection in my life. Preoccupied with buying a hideaway cottage in Ireland, where I had lived as a child, I realised I was on a quest for the enchantment that I had once known. Nostalgically, I envisaged the lush green hills and dales of a country that was once known as the Island of Saints and Scholars. Ireland has birthed many renowned poets, writers, storytellers and musicians who have bared their souls to share their universally resonant narratives. 'Surely I could satisfy my desire for inner riches in the Emerald Isle?' I thought.

'How about writing the enchanted story of your life?' suggested Nick. I agreed, certain that I'd run out of material after a short anecdote or two.

That evening I began writing a blog of tales drawn from my life. Often a story would surface as a vague memory – an image or a feeling – yet, as I wrote them down, each one emerged with its own form, energy and wisdom.

It quickly became clear to me from the responses to the blog that people resonated with the themes of the stories, finding them beguiling, and that they were even inspired by them to excavate their own lives in order to discover their own wisdom.

The first twenty narratives flowed easily but then I got stuck. Despite more than forty years on the planet, I had literally exhausted the enchanting anecdotes that I believed were worth sharing. As I dug deeper I began to lose my confidence: 'Nobody really wants to read about the difficult times – do they? I dealt with the dark days at the time, so why would I want to parade them now as entertainment?'

However, American mythologist Joseph Campbell once said: 'Where you stumble, there lies your treasure. The very cave you are afraid to enter turns out to be the very source of what you are looking for'.

Beneath the darkness the wisdom is buried.

By sheer chance I discovered that there are people out there who entertain audiences by performing stories – and so I decided to train as a storyteller and turn my tales into a performing art. Encouraged by my training to tell the raw stories, I made my debut by engaging the audience with a story of mine called 'Toasting the Priest', which you will find later in the book. I walked nervously onto the stage.

The room was quiet as I surveyed the assembly of fifty or so story enthusiasts from the local community.

'I grew up in Ireland where it's lush and green and rains two days out of three,' I began. Soon people were punctuating my story with laughter in all the right places, so I relaxed. Then we came to the song that I had rehearsed as a means of inviting audience participation: 'Another Brick in the Wall' by Pink Floyd.

'Will you sing it with me?' I asked.

The audience responded with a resounding 'yes!' and I gestured for them to stand. Everyone got up and stamped their feet, marching into an allegorical sausage machine – mimicking the video from the 1980s that was innovative in its time. My husband, David, played guitar, strumming out the major and minor cords to keep us on beat and in tune. We sang, 'we don't need no education' which was ironic since the performance was being held in a college! The applause was rapturous and as the song finished I was euphoric.

However, the story wasn't finished. The next step was risky, but now I knew that I could confidently navigate the listeners towards the darker side of the tale – the dangerous territory. Bravely, they journeyed with me into a place of heartbreak and reverently became as quiet as they had been raucous only a few moments earlier. Every eye and ear courageously followed the furrows of the unfolding narrative until it was time to return to the lightness again. Eventually we moved into laughter, which was wildly enchanting as it reverberated around the quaint wooden storytelling hut. We had traversed undulant terrain together. And I had experienced a palpable shift in consciousness, knowing now that I could transmute the dark days into stories containing universal truths that could inspire others.

Upon my return home from the storytelling sabbatical, I excavated my memories for gems of wisdom and wrote a collection of life stories, many of which have made it into this book. Like a box of assorted chocolates, some are light and bubbly, others are rich and dark with a bitter-sweet kick; some are deliciously mouth melting, while others are a delightful surprise.

Despite the fact that I've been a personal development enthusiast and journaling fan since my twenties, writing these vignettes was powerfully cathartic for me. Each story had a beginning, middle and an end, encapsulating a life stage. In every narrative a meaning or several were revealed. Many characters emerged – villains, heroes and angels. The wisdom I acquired from mining these stories could never have been gleaned from any workshop or course – only from recognising the gifts in my personal history. But we all have these characters in our lives, so let's be grateful for what we learn through our experiences with them, because some of our most troublesome relationships are with those who are in fact our best teachers.

During the many years in which I worked on my personal development, I revisited times gone by, accepting and healing experiences that were difficult. I didn't care to linger on them and I was grateful that they were behind me. While I had made peace with them, I hadn't embraced them yet as treasures. But, by exploring these stories further, I discovered the joy of honouring my own history, rather than merely accepting it. It took me beyond acceptance to appreciating my life experiences as precious gifts of wisdom that could inspire others. Accepting, honouring, loving and learning from your personal stories so that you can create more empowering stories in the future, is the message of this book.

The stories I tell are based upon the meanings that I attached to my life experiences both at the time they occurred and later – from a perspective gleaned through time, maturity and shifting consciousness.

These stories are true. However, let me qualify that statement: they are my truth today in the same way that everyone's stories are just that – their own truths. Stories evolve as our awareness shifts, so we won't always tell them in exactly the same way.

There were times that I didn't want to revisit. It seemed simpler to keep them locked away in distant memory, but when I did commit them to the page, I found that it was powerfully healing. Reframing them with new perspectives was freeing. When I discovered the humour, the poignancy and the gifts from my stories, I took them more lightly and treasured the wisdom they revealed.

You too have a rich repertoire of life stories, regardless of whether you have buried them deep within your psyche or brought them into your awareness and come to appreciate their wisdom. When you decide to embrace your own stories, extract their gems of wisdom and appreciate their gifts – you can expect to gain a richer sense of your own identity and purpose and recognise the beauty and enchantment of your life. The process will transform your energy and relationships. As the novelist Tom Robbins said, 'It's never too late to have a happy childhood.'

But it isn't just our childhood stories that offer wisdom. Everyday, we craft our reality by articulating our experiences and interactions with others.

And stories can be rewritten regardless of when they happened in our lives – it's a matter of revisiting them and acknowledging any pain we have about the events they describe. Then we can expand our awareness and reframe our interpretation of events. This is not in order to pretend that those experiences didn't happen, or to gloss over how challenging they may have been, but to understand the bigger picture. What were the people involved trying to achieve (rightly or wrongly)? And what did we learn? How has the experience shaped us? What significance does it hold now for the way in which we choose to live our lives in the future?

It is never too late to change our perspective and we can often bring a whole new meaning to a set of facts when we revisit them, thereby creating a different story. With distance things change. We are able to laugh at our past foibles when at the time we were mortified by them; we can find wisdom in the rubble of a shattered dream. New learning emerges that might enable us to anchor ourselves in the world in a more empowering way, building a richer sense of personal identity and greater clarity about our purpose in life.

When we become expert at reframing our stories, at retrieving our gifts from their hiding places, at laughing at ourselves, at appreciating poignant moments and being grateful for the smallest kindnesses, that is when we can transform our personal histories into inspiring works of art. In exactly the same way that a master sculptor can take an ordinary rock and carve an amazing sculpture, we can transform seemingly mundane, even unpalatable, life stories into the richest art and learning for the future.

Turning your life stories into art can become a way of life, yet it takes daily effort to avoid getting drawn into the cynical mindset that is pervasive in our society. There are tools and techniques at the end of each story in this book that are designed to help you carve away the dark cynicism and allow the light of enchantment, or the Tao of your story, to touch your heart and soul. You might find it helpful to record your responses in a special journal.

Discover your treasure:

1. Choose an event from your own past. Tell a story with a beginning, middle and an end about it to yourself now.

2. Can you think of examples where your story about the situation might be different to someone else's?

3. How do you feel about the idea that your stories are simply your truth based upon the filters you're viewing them through?

4. How do you feel about the idea that you can change your perspective and, in so doing, completely change the story that you're telling?

5. Think about a time when you told yourself a story about something and then came across new information which meant that you changed your perspective about it; e.g. somebody said or did something that hurt you and you realised later that the person was in a difficult place at the time, which meant that you could now empathise with them again.

6. How did it make you feel to be able to tell yourself a more empowering story about the situation?

7. How could it enhance your life if you were to consider the stories that you tell yourself on a regular basis and consciously ask if there might be a more empowering, perspective that you could take?

2. BLESSED BELIEFS

I'll never forget the sheer horror on Granny's face that spring day in 1970 as we watched my brother's antics. We were in the living room of my family's house on our farm in the West of Ireland. Granny (my Mum's mother) was a small, broad shouldered woman with wiry, chin length, grey hair which she wore pulled back in a clip. She always wore a tunic to keep her clothes clean and several cardigans. Two pairs of flesh coloured stockings held up with elastic garters kept her legs warm. Her practical and grounded nature was personified further in her size eight feet. She preferred men's shoes for everyday wear to accommodate her corns and bunions, unlike the shiny, stylish pair she wore to church.

Granny was a devoutly religious woman who attended Mass on Sunday despite hail, rain or snow. She said her rosary morning and night, twiddling her beads between her fingers as her lips moved silently. I'd often get into Granny's bed in the morning and she'd tell me all about God and heaven and hell.

'Heaven,' she said, 'is a place you go if you've been good and you live there happily forever and ever with God. Hell,' she said, 'is a place you go if you've been bad and you burn there forever with the devil. You go to purgatory if you've been middling – neither good nor bad – and you stay there until God decides that you're good enough for heaven.'

'What happens in purgatory?' I asked.

'There's a fire there too,' she said.

Oh no! I knew I shouldn't have asked – I didn't want to hear that answer. Aged nearly four, I struggled anxiously to know if I was good enough for God.

Granny lived with us and cared for my brother William and me when our Mum was teaching at the local primary school. Apart from scaring the living day lights out of me with stories of hell and purgatory, Granny was great. She was kind and jolly, with the heartiest laugh. I loved sitting on her lap and snuggling in while she'd hold me tight and tell me a story.

Granny melded into her corner armchair, sewing or knitting, while William and I had tremendous freedom to play and improvise. William was a two year old, rambunctious toddler with a mop of curly, mid-brown hair. He had a passion for dismantling things that he was unable to reassemble. His favourite innovation was morphing the dining room chairs into a car. Together, we'd turn them onto their backs, laying the seat pads in front of them. He'd take the driver's seat and say, 'Brm, brm, brm,' while I was parked in the passenger's pew.

Click-click! Granny's needles deftly added inches to her knitting. Occasionally quietness would fall between the rows and she'd glance over her spectacles at us before continuing to knit one, purl one. Chaos abounded in the room but Granny was blind to it. Our joy and happiness mattered more than order – until she'd check the time and say, 'tidy-up now before she comes home,' so that our Mum didn't walk into bedlam after her day at school.

One grey and cloudy day, William and I were on the rampage and our pandemonium was palpable. We had abandoned the car in favour of an unlocked cupboard that was normally out of bounds for mischievous little hands. Carefully, we opened the cupboard and discovered a virtual Aladdin's cave containing all of manner of random objects, such as haberdashery, books, string and candles.

In sheer glee, we began to empty the cupboard contents onto the floor and – as we did so – a tall, thin, cream tallow candle rolled across the floor towards William. He grabbed it and began to wield it like a sword.

Granny carried on knitting calmly in the corner armchair – click, click, click – she whipped the wool around the needles.

William boisterously decided to pitch his new toy against an armchair. Whack! The candle came down forcefully against the chair. Whack, whack, whack! – he was now vigorously beating the chair with the candle.

Granny glanced round sharply and threw down her knitting as she exited her armchair, an expression of sheer horror on her face. She stumbled across the room, weaving her way through our playtime debris. 'God almighty!' she exclaimed. 'Look what he's doing with the blessed candle.' Granny made the sign of the cross.

No ordinary candle was at stake here. This one had been blessed by the Church and was deemed to be sacred. Granny wrestled the blessed candle from my brother, saving it, the chair and my brother's soul. I was stunned into silence, certain that a sin had been committed and that my brother's act was sure to provoke the wrath of God. Having had his toy confiscated, William was angry. I was bewildered and fearful, knowing what I did about heaven, hell and purgatory. Our playtime had turned into a drama. And while we soon forgot about the blessed candle, moving on to new mischief, the message not to mess with sacred things for fear of God's fury stayed with me until I came to know a different truth about the nature of the Universe.

In our Irish Catholic family, God was a significant and capricious character. If you were good he was kindly and loving, but he didn't suffer fools gladly. You had to keep a check on yourself and repent if you had done wrong lest you be punished.

That was how Granny had been indoctrinated as a girl. Priests were regarded as men of power – God's apostles on earth. Later, the way that religion was taught in schools changed and children were taught that heaven is being with God and that hell is when we're separated from God. That was certainly a healthier concept to teach to small children. My Mum taught children a notion of heaven on earth in which the difference between being in heaven with God or separated from God was determined by whether you showed love. Now I know that she was right in her assertion that love connects people, but as a small child I wasn't sure whether Granny's story or Mum's was true. Granny's story was certainly more powerful and frightening to my malleable child's mind.

For years, I held on to those fire and brimstone beliefs deep within my psyche and continued to evaluate myself and everything else around me as good, middling or bad, while anxious that the consequences for being anything other than good could be dire. In time, I came to relinquish the idea of God as a bearded man in the sky, but I still found it hard to believe in a benevolent Universe – unless you were good. The good, bad and middling construct remained, and I believed that everything had to be earned, including love. As an adult, I was able to recognise that my beliefs had been shaped by ideas designed to control people and keep them on the straight and narrow. However, it has taken me many more years to shake off the concept that love has to be earned by being good and to believe instead that the Universe or God – or whatever we wish to call a power greater than ourselves – loves us unconditionally.

Significantly, I also learned to have a fear of authority figures from this experience. For years, I didn't understand where those fears came from. My cognitive mind would rationalise the fears away, but they were held at a deeper level within my psyche. While respect for authority is important if we are to avoid society disintegrating into lawlessness, fear of authority is not healthy. We need to be able to question and challenge people who are in authority because in a democracy, after all, they are there only because we put them there.

Reflecting on what happened that day, I recognise that the story I tell is from the perspective of my four-year-old mind. I didn't know what was going on in Granny's mind. She may have believed that abusing the candle was blasphemous or she might have simply wanted us to show respect for its sacredness. Granny might have been worried that William would damage the chair or hit me with the candle as I was standing next to him.

Today, however, when I picture my curly-haired brother hitting the chair vigorously with his 'toy' and Granny exclaiming, 'God almighty, look what he's doing with the blessed candle', as she stumbles across the debris that we had strewn all over the floor, it brings a smile to my face. It's a real-life comedy scene and I love it – what a gift!

Discover your treasure:

1. What resonates with you about this story?

Our beliefs about the Universe or God (or whatever deities we do or don't acknowledge) profoundly affect the way we live.

2. What are your beliefs about your relationship with the Universe, God or a power that's greater than yourself?

3. Are your relationships with authority similar or different?

4. Can you trace your beliefs back to your childhood?

5. What stories come to mind?

6. How do these beliefs serve you in your life?

7. Are there any more empowering stories and beliefs that you'd like to replace or enhance these with that might serve you better?

3. THUMB WAR

One, two, three, FOUR – that's the age at which I declared Thumb War.

'Achoo, achoo!' Every morning I crawled out of bed and shuffled in my pyjamas to my chair at the kitchen table, my Shirley Temple curls in a bedraggled mop after a good night's sleep. Breakfast was a hard-boiled egg with toast that always made me sneeze, sending small pieces of egg flying across the table. But as I was only four years old nobody minded – my father always laughed and said, 'Bless you!'

Left behind me in bed was a motley crew of cuddly toys and dolls that I had amassed to befriend me at night. Amongst them were a scruffy grey dog, a pristine teddy in a pink satin dress and a beautiful doll with silky blond hair whose blue eyes closed when I laid her down to sleep. I often shared my pillow with up to eleven little friends, which would leave me struggling to find space for my head on the pillow too. Then I'd curl up, suck my thumb and sleep safe and sound with my merry tribe.

On my fourth birthday my father said, 'Would you like to go to school?' I said, 'Yes,' not knowing what school would be like. A few weeks later, I sat nervously in the car with my Mum and my older sister, Mary, who was aged five and a half. My brown satchel hung on my back, as I anticipated my first day in the classroom. Sadly, my furry friends weren't allowed to come with me but my Mum assured me that I would make new friends there.

School was confusing as everyone called my Mum, Miss. 'Should I call her Mum or Miss?' I wondered, before deciding, 'better to call her Miss like everyone else does.'

Which was how my Mum became two people: Mum at home and Miss at school – except for lunchtime when she became Mum again as my sister and I ate lunch with her. And so, as I watched her teaching at the front of the class, with the elegance of a porcelain doll, she was my Mum and yet she wasn't Mum.

Ours was a two-teacher school with less than forty pupils dotted across eight classes. As there was no special day of the year on which to start school, I was the only new kid on my first day and there was only one other girl in my class. Two boys joined a few months later.

Being the teacher's child, I was expected to be a beacon of good behaviour. That was a struggle for me at the age of four. While Mum morphed into the teacher, I sucked my thumb and twirled a playful curl as I voyaged in my mind to places more magical than the mundane classroom. Staring through the big sash windows and drifting away to the land of make-believe was enticing to me, while staying present in the classroom was dull.

My Mum, in her teacher personality, was baffled when it came to engaging my wayward mind. She complained to my father about my lack of attention in class: 'It's because she's sucking her thumb all day that she's not listening at school.'

He turned to me and said, 'If you don't stop sucking your thumb I will put something horrible on it and you won't want to suck it anymore.' I blinked, frightened and anxious. When I climbed into bed later, my sense of foreboding refused to subside. Even the teddies and dolls couldn't make it go away.

Morning arrives and I shuffle into the kitchen as usual in my pale yellow pyjamas. While my Mum prepares breakfast, my father polishes his shoes. Suddenly I'm grabbed. My father pulls me towards him and smears black polish all over my thumbs. I hear a scream. It's my own voice. I'm shocked, angry and shrieking hysterically. My yellow pyjama top becomes streaked in black polish as I rub my thumbs on it and run to the bathroom to wash my hands. As the tap streams, tears roll down my cheeks.

When I return to the kitchen both my mother and sister look awkward. My brother comes running in to see what's happening, always excited by a good story. He rushes to my grandmother's bedroom and tells her, and she laughs.

Yet the tears are still running down my face and nobody is comforting me. I feel a mixture of emotions – anger, betrayal, humiliation, fear and abandonment.

I decide, 'I can't trust people; even my family don't love or care about me.' I declare 'Thumb War'.

After that I became insecure, on edge and hyperaware. Thumb sucking became my secret night-time comfort, together with the reassuring presence of the teddy bear with the silk dress, the scruffy grey dog and the beautiful doll. 'They would never betray me,' I thought. But by shutting the door to my heart to protect myself from being hurt, I had unwittingly limited the space for enchantment to enter and so life was a shade darker for me after that.

This story remained locked away in my memory until I grew up and had the opportunity to air it in the safe surroundings of a healing workshop. To heal the scratch on my soul, I went back in time, floating above the event and even tasting the pain briefly in order to reconnect with it. I knew in that moment that parents can make silly mistakes, often with the most positive intentions. As a child of the Universe, I realised that I could never have been abandoned: the separation I felt had resulted from the decision I'd made not to trust people but to paddle my own canoe instead. I realised that it was no mere coincidence that my thumbs were the focus of the incident, because the distinctively human opposable thumb represents the ego – the part of us that is separate from others; hence it was a Thumb War.

Heaven, like my mother used to say, is when you show love and are open and connected. Hell is turning away from love and shutting the door. When we close our hearts to people, even if we feel they deserve it, we shut down our spiritual connection and our intuition, swapping them instead for anxiety and fear.

During my healing session, a state of expanded consciousness afforded me greater insights into the minds of my family in that childhood scene. I understood that, besides relieving their own irritation at my behaviour, intentions such as ensuring that I would learn well at school and have straight teeth lay behind my parent's desire to stop my thumb-sucking. I was able to forgive and, as I did, my connection to creative consciousness strengthened and I could see that I always had the choice to reconnect to the power and wisdom of the Universe. It was time to declare a truce on Thumb War.

Then I melted into bliss and I began to laugh. At first it was just a little and then more laughter came, until eventually I was laughing so hard that tears ran down my face and my sides ached. It was overwhelming and I couldn't articulate precisely what was so funny. My body rocking with hilarity, I wriggled about in my chair to get comfortable as I could no longer sit upright. I had bounced into the bliss that comes with powerful moments of reconnection to creative consciousness.

In revisiting the story, I had entered the dark cave and discovered a crock of gold. Light that had been eclipsed was now streaming back into my life. I had recaptured some of that elusive enchantment to take with me on the next steps of my life's journey.

The message here is not about how to be a perfect parent – it is a story about how to heal our hearts when we have felt hurt. Having a healthy trust in people is imperative to having good relationships. Being hurt by other people's behaviour is the stuff of life – it happens to everyone and often it is so subtle that we don't know why we have become less trusting, more suspicious and fearful, or why our world has become a less enchanting place. For some people, these experiences can be traumatic, in which case counselling and support may be necessary – so seek help. If your story is not quite so traumatic, you might find it useful to explore how an early decision not to trust people might be affecting your life today. You can reclaim your bliss by acknowledging these dark places, healing your heart and forgiving those people who may have hurt you unintentionally by simply not thinking through their actions towards you.

Discover your treasure:

1. What resonates with you about this story?
2. How open is your heart – how trusting are you of people?
3. Do you recall a time in your life when you decided not to trust people?
4. How old were you? Who was involved? How did you feel?
5. How is that decision affecting your life now?

6. What would the older, wiser you tell that younger version of yourself now?

7. What would it take for you to let go of that story, forgive the people involved and open your heart again?

8. Would you be prepared to change that story now?

4. A STITCH IN TIME

A ll the time I had spent clicking my plastic red needles should have resulted in a long strip of knitting – but it didn't. My work hadn't grown beyond the four rows that had been done to get me started.

At school we learned crafts: painting, drawing, collage, sewing and knitting. Knitting was by far the hardest. My first project was a hair band – a length of garter stitch with the ends sewn together. I began with a ball of lavender wool that was left over from one of Granny's knitting assignments.

At school, ten stitches were cast on to the needles by my Mum and she showed me how to knit a few rows before handing it over to me. Despite an afternoon of knitting at school, I was disappointed to see that my efforts weren't turning into a hair band as I had intended. When I looked around, I noticed that the results of other people's endeavours were growing while mine was static. 'Maybe I need to knit faster?' I thought. So I continued even more ferociously than before.

In the evening, I confessed to Granny, 'My hair band isn't getting any longer and I don't know what to do.'

She took the little red needles from me and began to construct row after row – making about ten rows in all. 'There you are,' she said, 'you just have to keep going.'

'Thanks, Granny,' I said and continued to click, click, click – hoping that eventually a hair band would appear. But still I made no progress.

The next day at school, I showed my knitting to my Mum and she said, 'Yes, good, that's coming on well.' I didn't admit that it was Granny's work and that I remained unable to knit. I kept it a secret because I was ashamed that I couldn't do something which seemed to come easily to everyone else.

Then, one evening, an old school friend of my Mum's called Nancy came to visit us with her sister, Bridie. I always talked to guests, enjoying the connection and the attention. While my Mum chatted with Nancy, Bridie spoke with me. She was dressed in a pink outfit with her hair piled on top of her head and asked me friendly questions such as, 'What do you like to play?' When I told her, she seemed so interested that I ran off to my bedroom and brought back a selection of toys to show her. She duly examined the teddy bear in the pink silk dress, the scruffy grey dog and the blue-eyed doll, and said, 'They're beautiful.' When I showed her how the red metal spinning top worked, I could tell that she was impressed, saying, 'Oh, isn't that lovely!'

By now we were firm friends and I trusted her, so I told her, 'I'm knitting a hair band at school – would you like to see it?' I ran off to get it and returned with the little red needles, the lavender ball of wool and the partly knitted rows of hair band.

'Oh, isn't that just great!' she said.

Then, I confided in her. 'Granny did that,' I said. 'When I knit, it doesn't work.'

'Really?' she said. 'Well, let me help you.' Then she took me on her knee and asked me to show her how I did my knitting. 'Ah, well that's great,' she said. 'Now let me show you a little trick.' She carefully held my hands over the needles and showed me how to pull a new loop each time I knitted into a stitch: 'In the needle, up the thread and out the new loop...'

I hadn't understood that I had to pull the new loop through each time. Although I had been making a grand display, gesticulating with the wool wrapped around my index finger, I'd simply been moving the stitches from one needle to the other and so it had been impossible for me to make any progress despite the tremendous effort I'd been investing. I tried this new way and it worked like magic. I thanked Bridie and knitted with her to show that I understood and could do it. The lavender wool was now quickly being transformed into a hair band.

My realisation that there was a knack to knitting marked the beginning of a creative journey that produced a variety of hair bands, scarves, tablemats, even a stuffed rabbit and eventually a sweater when I was older.

Today, when I have the sense that I'm metaphorically moving the stitches from one needle to the other, investing effort that's not generating results, I remind myself that 'there's a knack to knitting' – as there is to everything else too.

It often takes courage to admit that, despite our best efforts, progress in some areas of our lives might have come to a halt. When we compare ourselves with others whom we think are further forward, we can be left feeling inadequate and ashamed. Rather than asking for the help that would catalyse us to a new level of success, we might pretend that everything is perfect and reassure ourselves that since we're putting in the hours we must eventually prevail.

In Neurolinguistic Programming (NLP), there is the supposition that if one person can do something then anyone using the same methodology can do it too. It's known as 'modelling excellence'. We can get stuck for a variety of reasons such as simply not knowing how to do something. Then we create an additional problem for ourselves: afraid of being labelled as incapable, we strive to protect our identities as competent people and therefore refuse to admit that we need help. This in turn leads to a third problem: our despondency that we're not getting results from our efforts leads us to question both our purpose and the fairness of the Universe, as we ask ourselves, 'Why am I here and what am I supposed to be doing with my life?'.

The way forward lies in recognising where our ego is stopping us from asking for help or from accepting the help that's available to us. It can be humbling for us to be vulnerable enough to admit that we're stuck and we don't know what to do. Yet it is liberating to find the right person who has the empathy and wisdom to listen and empower us. We don't come into the world able to do everything. We're compelled to share our pieces of the puzzle in order to help each other to solve life's riddles. Whether we're stuck in a difficult relationship with someone or with a seemingly impossible task, or we find ourselves confronting something that is as yet nameless which seems to be foiling our success, it pays to ask for help.

I'm always amazed at what happens when I have the humility to tell someone whom I trust that something isn't working for me. I might not even know what lies behind the problem, yet I feel that I 'should' be able to deal with it by myself. Then I remember what I learned as a child: 'There's a knack to knitting.' We all have blind spots and find ourselves caught up in waves and stormy seas which we need other people's help to navigate. Often, the perfect person is available to help us, yet we ignore them, preferring to keep trying by ourselves. We could decide instead to open ourselves to those people who possess the pieces of life's mystery that are different to ours. I have found that they are usually delighted to give us the time and attention we need to help us grow.

Remember the old proverb: *A stitch in time saves nine.* So be courageous and ask for the help you need now.

Discover your treasure:
1. What resonates with you about this story?
2. Is there any area of your life or work that seems to be stuck right now?

3. How much time, have you invested in trying harder?
4. How does trying harder without achieving results leave you feeling?
5. What stories have you told yourself about this situation and how do these serve you or hinder you?
6. How do you feel about asking people for help?
7. What could you do differently to create the change you want?
8. Who could you ask to help you now?

5. WARRIOR WISDOM

When I was five years old, I spent more hours than other infants at school as I would wait until my Mum had finished teaching the older kids so that I could go home with her. One day she said, 'Claire, because you're in the infant class you can walk home by yourself at half-past two if you like. Would you like to do that?'

It sounded exciting and scary as it would mean walking the one-and-half mile journey by myself. I pondered the idea and then declared, 'I'll do it – I'll walk home from school on my own.'

At half-past two the next day, I packed my satchel, ready to go home. My Mum undid the latch on the school door and held my hand as we walked down the path towards the gate. We crossed the stile beside the school gate and waited while a car and a lorry rolled past. I could see that the road was clear on both sides as Mum pressed me to look right, left and then right again. I ran across the road and waved goodbye to her as I started the stroll home. It wasn't a busy road – cars went by and the occasional truck. Along it, there were two small farm cottages on the left-hand side – one inhabited, the other derelict – and a public house on the right. Eventually, I came to a T-junction where I turned right into the single-track road that led to our house.

It was a warm spring day as I trotted along, taking in the lush green fields, the stone walls, the bushes, trees and wildflowers. Birds chirped merrily and it was a delightful walk. Farmers occasionally passed on their tractors and waved to me, and I responded in kind. In the Irish countryside, people greet you even when they aren't sure who you are. That way, you can be certain that you haven't inadvertently ignored someone you should recognise, living in a small community.

As I floated along in the sunshine without a care, a voice startled me. 'How is the girleen?' it said from behind a stone wall. I stopped and turned to see who was speaking. A man stood there with a flat cap, holding a pitchfork. Farmers used these to turn over the hay they made from dried grass that they saved as winter fodder for their livestock.

'I'm fine, thank you,' I replied.

'Are you on your way home from school?'

'Yes, I am!'

'And who will be waiting for you at home?

'Granny and Daddy,' I said.

'And will your dinner be ready when you get home?'

'No, I'll have dinner later when Mum gets home.'

Then he said, 'I'll tell you what you'll do' – a great Irish phrase – 'When you get home, sit at the table and bang on it with your knife and fork, and say, "Where's my dinner?"'

I stood on the other side of the stone wall with my satchel on my back, nodding politely while thinking, 'That's the silliest thing I've ever heard – and he's a grown-up.' Out loud, I said, 'I have to go now.'

'Goodbye, girleen! Don't forget!' he shouted after me.

'Goodbye,' I replied, waving as I continued up the hill. I passed a field with a chestnut shire horse in it and then on and on I walked, until eventually I turned into our driveway. I was delighted with myself for having walked all the way home as I made my way up the drive and opened the door, where Granny was waiting for me.

'How was your walk?' Granny asked.

'Well, it was nice and then I spoke to this man – and do you know what he said to me?'

'Tell me!'

So I shared the story of the man on the other side of the stone wall. And we laughed together.

It soon became usual for me to walk home. One day, I had passed the field where the man with the pitchfork had spoken to me and was heading towards the hill when I realised that the shire horse who lived in the field was unusually close to the stone wall. Then I saw stones strewn along the ditch at the roadside and that's when I noticed that the wall had partially collapsed. As I walked up the hill, the shire horse ambled towards the gap in the wall and slowly made his way onto the road. 'Oh my, God,' I thought, 'he's enormous – much bigger than most grown-ups, let alone me.' I felt my heart pounding in my chest. 'Shall I walk past him, or maybe if I wait he'll go back into the field again?'

The huge horse started to graze on the grassy verge, showing no sign of going back into the field. Halting my stride, I stood contemplating my next move. He seemed engrossed in eating the lush grass and oblivious to me. 'I have to get home,' I reasoned to myself. 'Maybe he won't notice if I just walk past quickly?' I braced myself, feigned bravery and focused beyond the shire horse to where I wanted to be. As I walked forward his immenseness loomed terrifyingly. Yet there was a calmness and gentleness to the beast.

As I placed one black patent shoe in front of the other I breathed deeply. The next thing, there I was, walking along behind him, aware of his magnificence. His tail swished gently and, when I was almost past him, he took a step backwards. 'Oh, my goodness!' My heart leapt and fortunately my legs kept churning out the steps. I wanted to run but something inside me said, 'Walk – don't run, don't startle him.'

As I made it beyond him relief washed over me. Yet I continued walking so that I could get around the next bend and out of sight of the horse. Finally I was there – exhausted and relieved that I had made it to a safer place. Soon I was turning into the driveway to our house and when I got home Granny was waiting for me.

'How was your walk home today?' she asked.

And so I told her all about getting beyond the majestic shire horse who had escaped from the field through the broken stone wall.

She listened curiously and said, 'You're home safe and well now.'

Mostly, the walk home from school was quiet and peaceful with almost nobody around. Then one day I had almost reached home when a truck with a trailer came rattling along behind me and I stepped onto the grassy verge to let it pass by. The driver stopped. Three men were inside the cab and the window was rolled down.

'Are you on your way home from school?' the driver asked.

'Yes,' I replied.

'Would you like a lift home?'

'No, thank you – I just live there,' I said, pointing to my house, which was about two hundred yards away, with the chimney top barely visible.

'Who's your father?' he asked. I told him, knowing that everybody knew everybody in the countryside. 'Ah!' he said. 'We know your father, so why don't you jump in and we'll give you a lift home.' I felt uncomfortable and I wanted these people to go away. The driver tried to persuade me: 'But sure, we know your father, we'll drop you at your house.'

I felt a sense of power in my body and a determination that rooted me to the ground. 'No,' I said, 'I want to walk home.'

With that he shrugged his shoulders, said, 'Okay,' rolled up the window and drove on.

I was relieved as I walked the last stretch home. Granny was there, waiting for me, and I told her about the men in the truck, but this time I told my Dad as well, because the encounter had disturbed me.

He asked, 'What did they look like and what kind of truck was it?'

I explained as best I could and he pondered, trying to work out if he knew these people. He didn't seem to be too perturbed so I tucked it away in my memory and I never saw the three men again.

There were no more adventures on the single-track road. As I grew older I stayed in school all day and either went home with my Mum or walked with my sister and the other kids.

That was then and I have found since that life is full of adventures in which we have to rely on our Inner Warrior. As children, we don't have rich life experiences to draw upon for decision-making. We only have our gut feelings and a few well remembered messages from our parents, such as, 'Look before you cross the road,' and, 'Don't talk to strangers.' At the age of five, I drew strength from my Inner Warrior, who didn't grapple with the burden of intellectualising everything but relied on intuition instead. You can't reason with an enormous shire horse when you're a child, or with adults, because you're not as confident and articulate as them – it's only a few years since you learned to speak. You can only use your instinct and trust that your Inner Warrior (who is more majestic than any shire horse) will tell you what to do next.

Today, I still do my best to listen to my Inner Warrior, although it's not always easy to distinguish between the many voices of fear, ego, guilt and bravado, and to recognise the voice of truth among them. Yet that voice is always there for us, looking out for us, whispering in our ear and guiding us everyday. It comes to each of us in different ways, be it a feeling in our bodies, a voice or image in our minds, or just through a sense of knowing. Our Inner Warrior looks beyond the demons and the distractions and remains focused on where we want to go and it will find a way to take us there, if we trust it.

We're in touch with our instinctive nature as children, but when we grow older our wise Inner Warrior can become dumbed down, as our intellect makes life more complicated for us by weighing up the pros and the cons of every situation, and by refusing to trust our intuition. We can end up confused, because our Inner Warrior knows the answer and wants to respond accordingly, while our minds can over think us into shrivelling, doubtful wrecks.

There are practices that can help us: these include meditation, exercise, making time to nourish our souls with things that inspire us, as well as basic self-nurturing activities such as drinking plenty of water and eating healthily to ensure that we're connected to our own instinctively wise Inner Warrior. So let's each nurture our Inner Warrior and trust it to guide our life's journey.

Discover your treasure:

1. What resonates with you about this story?
2. How connected are you to your Inner Warrior – your innate sense of knowingness and wisdom?
3. Consider a time when you knew your own mind, heart and soul in the face of persuasion and you listened to yourself and followed your instincts?
4. How did that inner wisdom come to you – was it an inner voice, an image, a feeling?
5. Where in your body was that sense of knowingness located?
6. What was the benefit of following your inner wisdom in that situation?
7. How connected are you to your inner wisdom today?
8. What practices might help you to gain clarity and reconnect with your Inner Warrior?

6. TRUSTING THE DANCE

In the midst of the hustle and bustle of the Feis, a dance gala held in a school gym, I heard my name being bellowed out over the public address system for the next dance.

'Why are they calling me?' I wondered. The next dance was an Irish reel and I hadn't practised that in the run-up to the Feis. I was frozen to the spot. 'How does it go – one, two, three and two, two, three?' I struggled to remember in the din of the gym, with my heart beating wildly and my mind drawing a blank. It was the first dance I'd learned when I began the classes eighteen months earlier. Now I was expected to go on stage in front of everyone and dance a reel. 'It must be a mistake.'

I had started going to Irish dancing classes with my sister Mary when I was aged four; and now I was six. Mum drove us to the school where the dance classes were held on a Saturday morning in a classroom where the desks had been pushed back to open up the floor space. As soon as we arrived, we slipped into our soft, black dancing shoes, laced them around our ankles and joined the class.

Our teacher, Mrs Fitzpatrick, had blonde curly hair and spoke in a strong voice that we could hear above the music. The Irish reel was the first dance that she taught us, demonstrating the steps by dancing with deliberation and checking that we had all grasped the footwork before playing the music. The music was fast and initially we struggled to keep up with it; however, Mrs Fitzpatrick would call out the steps loudly to keep us on track. 'One, two, three and two, two, three,' she'd say. 'Toe and heel, girls. Speed it up, girls; slow it down, girls.'

After several months learning to perfect our Irish reel, we moved on to the jig, which meant new steps and a new rhythm to learn. While the reel was simple with 4/4 time beat, the jig had a more complicated 6/8 time rhythm. But after weeks of Mrs Fitzpatrick telling us, 'Kick out and back, and down two, three, four,' we eventually mastered that dance too.

After the jig, we stepped up to the three-hand reel, which we danced in a circle of three – as the name suggests. We joined our right hands together in the centre above our heads while we danced clockwise; then released our hands and danced uniformly between each other. The three-hand reel was fun.

The older kids had advanced to the hornpipe – a dance with presence. They had hard, shiny, black shoes that were laced or buckled at the front and had tapped soles, which they clattered against the floor like the performers do in Riverdance. I wanted a pair of those noisy shoes so that I could dance with the power and clarity of the hornpipe.

All these dances were performed standing bolt upright with our arms straight down by our sides. Only our legs were allowed to move, while the upper halves of our bodies remained motionless. We began every dance poised with right leg stretched forwards and toes pointed.

At home, Mary and I practised dancing to recordings of Irish music played on my parents' record player. We were aware of the upcoming Feis and increased our practice time. However, I didn't know which dance I might be performing. As a daydreaming six-year-old, I didn't ponder on practical matters such as which dance I would be doing at the Feis. Since I'd never been to a Feis, I had no concept of what it would be like and so it wasn't real to me.

Before the Feis, I practised the jig regularly at my sister's behest and I had the three-hand reel off to a tee. It was fresh in my mind from the class and that was what I expected to perform on the day.

The day of the Feis dawned and Mary and I wore the identical, white-magenta-and-purple check, pleated dresses that Mum had got a dressmaker to make for us. As we journeyed to the Feis, I was blissfully ignorant of what was about to happen there.

Upon our arrival, we got out of the car into a milling crowd of kids from several dance schools, all decked out in *de rigueur* Irish dancing embroidered dresses, with cream sashes draped over their shoulders, held in position with ostentatious Celtic broaches. The event opened with several groups of dancers skillfully executing their craft to the cheers of the audience and the nods of impressed adjudicators.

Then I heard my name called over the public address system. 'That's you, you have to dance a reel,' a friend standing close by whispered to me.

'But that's the one I *haven't* practised,' I thought. 'I can't remember the steps.'

Frozen on the spot and bewildered with fear, I glanced around to see if my Mum or sister were anywhere in sight. The music began to play, my cue to get on the stage and perform. Slowly, my legs began to move towards the front of the room, past the musicians' box. As I edged closer to the enormous stage, I stopped, looked up at it and gulped. Then I reluctantly climbed up the wooden steps to it. 'Oh boy, it's high up,' I thought. When I glanced down from my elevated position, the people in the audience seemed to have shrunk. I walked towards the middle of the stage, having no idea what I would do once I got there because I still couldn't remember a step of the reel. My tummy somersaulted as I caught sight of the adjudicating panel below. 'They're looking at me, waiting for me to do something,' I thought.

'Aw, all on her own!' I heard the Master of Ceremonies say over the microphone, and I realised that not only was I performing a dance I hadn't rehearsed, but I was one of the few people dancing by myself.

I stood poised in position, head, shoulders and body perfectly aligned, arms parallel to my sides, right foot extended and toes pointing towards the floor. 'So far so good,' I thought. The memory of Mrs Fitzpatrick's voice saying, 'One, two, three and two, two, three,' gave me the confidence to begin – but I had only a vague recollection of the steps that came next.

The little orchestra was now playing a traditional Irish reel in 4/4 time just for me – and so it was time to move. A room full of people were watching with interest, waiting for me to dance. Well, it was certainly going to be interesting since I couldn't remember the steps.

After the musical introduction, I kicked off with the few steps that I could recall. 'What am I going to do next?' I thought. Then, just as I was about to panic, I heard Mrs Fitzpatrick calling out the steps to me just like she did in class, but quietly. She had crept onto the stage and stood discreetly by the curtain. I danced to the reassuring sound of her voice.

Before I knew it, I was in my element on stage – at one with the orchestra and with Mrs Fitzpatrick's voice as she called out each step in perfect time for me to sustain the flow of the dance. As I continued, I began to recall the story of the dance not in my mind but in my body, in my muscle memory, and dancing became effortless. Around and around the stage I twirled, exhilarated as the reel reeled me.

Eventually, the music slowed and the dance finished. I walked to the edge of the stage, surveyed the crowd, bowed gracefully and absorbed the rapturous applause. Then I turned and walked back down the steps, feeling pleased with myself. The adjudicators realised that I didn't know the dance steps but commended my dancing for poise and grace anyway.

I was reminded of this narrative from my life repertoire when I did my training as a storyteller. One of our assignments was to recite a poem and my friend Rebecca brought along a beautiful piece from St Augustine, which spoke deeply to me about the limitations of our conscious minds when they tell us we can't do something. I am grateful for what I learned from the dance that day about the power of taking action, and trusting that all would come right. And thank you, Mrs Fitzpatrick, for being my angel!

I Praise The Dance

I praise the dance, for it frees people
from the heaviness of matter
and binds the isolated to community.

I praise the dance, which demands everything:
health and a clear spirit and a buoyant soul.

Dance is a transformation of space, of time, of people,
who are in constant danger of becoming all brain, will,
or feeling.

Dancing demands a whole person,
one who is firmly anchored in the centre of his life,

who is not obsessed by lust for people and things
and the demon of isolation in his own ego.

Dancing demands a freed person,
one who vibrates with the equipoise of all his powers.

I praise the dance.

O man, learn to dance, or else the angels in heaven will
not know what to do with you.

St Augustine

I could have run away rather than danced the reel that
day. Since I was only six years old, nobody would have
forced me to go on stage had I protested. Yet I didn't think
that refusing to dance was an option, even though I hadn't
practised the reel, didn't know the steps or have a clue
about what I would do on stage. The truth is that, crazy as
it sounds, it didn't even occur to me to walk away. It would
have been a sensible choice but I wasn't sensible, I was six.
The age of reason, which apparently happens from about
seven years old, hadn't inhibited me. So, although scared, I
stood boldly on the edge of the stage, waiting and trusting
the Universe to dance me.

I'm often inspired by early footage of people who have
since become masters of their craft, especially those in the
public gaze. We love to laugh at the mistakes they made
while they were finding their feet. The award-winning Irish
boy band, Boyzone, made their television debut dancing on
The Late Late Show on RTÉ in Ireland back in the early

1990s. They were a manufactured band, dubbed as Ireland's answer to the British boy band sensation Take That. Prior to their debut appearance on Irish TV, Boyzone had been a band for no more than twenty-four hours (following the results of the auditions for the band being announced) and had spent only thirty minutes rehearsing together. They came across as a group of delusional teenagers whose naïvety amused the audience. However, long before the band had sold twenty-five million records, people had stopped laughing at them and started loving their music and vocal talent. But it was only by having the courage to boldly go outside their comfort zone to begin with, that the group, like many of their ilk, became brilliant and successful.

We don't have to be seekers of fame and fortune to experience discomfort in the face of uncertainty. At the edge of any abyss – a challenge or a new beginning – it's good to know that as we dare to move forward and gather momentum, the Universe will join in and dance us. Human angels like Mrs Fitzpatrick will guide our journey. Muscle memory and subconscious knowledge will support our flow. We can be grateful and trust the dance.

As St Augustine says:

Oh man [or woman] learn to dance,
or else the angels in heaven will not know what to do with you.

Discover your treasure:

1. What resonates with you about this story?
2. What stories of trusting the dance, and going boldly forward despite uncertainty, can you recall from your own life?
3. What do you usually do when you don't know the next steps to take?
4. Do you hide, waiting for certainty, or move forward anyway?
5. What would happen if you moved boldly into the limelight of your life despite your uncertainty?
6. Would you be prepared to stumble with everybody watching you as you get into your stride?
7. Who is waiting in the shadows to help and support you in sustaining your flow?

7. MASTER CRAFTSWOMAN

My grandmother's dressmaking prowess was legendary. She was kind and stubborn in equal measure, qualities that made her a determined and tenacious woman who loved to serve others. Granny raised five daughters between the 1930s and the 1950s, the eldest born only after she'd had several miscarriages. According to local folk, her daughters were always beautifully dressed with wonderful hats – thanks to Granny's dressmaking talent. She also made dresses for local ladies with the fabric they supplied and never accepted any money from them.

Now in her seventies, Granny was less agile than in her younger years, so she happily alternated between her comfortable corner armchair and the manual foot-operated Singer sewing machine that must have been almost half a century old. Occasionally, I'd see her take a small metal canister of oil from the drawer and grease the wheel of the sewing machine, before whipping up her next creation. When she wasn't dressmaking she was knitting or crocheting, her bony hands working deftly and her hazel eyes following the process keenly through her brown-rimmed spectacles. Days of concentrated effort would result in a sweater, a cardigan or even a bolero to complement a dress that she had made earlier. Whatever she turned her creative hand to, turned out brilliantly.

Granny didn't make clothes for herself beyond what she called her 'bibs'. These were tunics made from navy cotton fabric with small flowers, which she wore over her clothes to keep them clean as she went about her day.

Everything else was made as a gift for someone she loved. My favourite dress was mauve patterned cotton with three pinch pleats in the front of the bodice, which she made for me when I was five. It was simple and beautiful and I enjoyed wearing it.

Mostly, Granny worked from dressmaking patterns, but at other times she worked straight from her imagination. My Mum would often borrow the huge pattern books from the fabric shop in town and we'd pore over them to decide what Granny would make us for the next season. Then my Mum would go shopping with a list for fabric, cotton thread, buttons and zips so that Granny could start work – and the next set of creations would be born.

She churned out these garments season after season like a possessed artist. It simply wasn't an option for her not to create and a lack of materials to work with made her antsy. In the absence of materials with which to make things, she would hunt around the house for garments that had been abandoned in wardrobes, so that she could dismantle and remodel them, giving them a new lease of life. With Granny in the house, if a discarded coat were ambitious to be a jacket or a skirt there was a distinct possibility that it would realise its dream.

I realised her unstoppable nature when I was six years old and my brother, William, was five. We were getting ready for school one morning, rushing around as Mum fussed to get us into the car. Granny called out to my brother. 'Come over here, I want to see you before you go to school,' she said. He didn't dare escape to school without attending to Granny. She was waiting in her armchair with her yellow tape measure in hand. 'Stand there,' she said. 'Arms out, turn around. Good! Now off you go to school.' William and I scampered to the car, where my Mum waited impatiently for us – she was a key holder and didn't want to leave children standing outside the school.

That day at school was unremarkable, and lessons pushed the morning's measuring episode to the back of my mind. It wasn't unusual for Granny to take people's vital statistics, although generally you knew what she was planning to make as you stretched out your arms and twirled around at her behest.

When school finished my Mum drove us home and we scrambled out of the car, dumping our satchels as we entered the house. Granny was smiling as she surveyed the room from her corner. 'William,' she called. He ran over to her. She held up a small, smart brown coat with a velvet collar and big brown buttons. 'What do you think?' she said.

William looked curiously at the coat. 'Where did you get that? Is it for me?' he asked.

'Yes,' said Granny, 'I made it for you. Put it on!' William took off his brown anorak and Granny held out the new coat as he slipped his arms into its sleeves. 'Turn around,' said Granny. He did.

By now, my Mum had entered the living room. 'Oh, that's lovely; it fits you just perfectly,' she said, on seeing William in Granny's creation. 'You can wear it to Mass on Sunday.'

William smiled, delighted with his new coat and agreed to wear it on Sunday. Granny was thrilled.

Then my Mum turned to her and said, 'I thought you said you didn't have any fabric – so how did you make that?'

Granny explained, 'I made it from an old coat of mine hanging up in the cloakroom. I hardly ever wore it; no point in having it there, going to waste.'

I had learned at school that God created the world from nothing and I thought, 'Granny is like that, she made a coat from almost nothing.' She had no pattern, no special fabric or shiny new buttons – just her genius, her passion and her desire to make something for somebody.

In his book *Outliers*, Malcolm Gladwell talks about the 10,000 hour rule: that it takes about 10,000 hours of practice to achieve mastery in any pursuit. Then in her seventies, Granny had been dressmaking all of her adult life and she had become a Master Craftswoman.

At the time of writing, it is weeks since Andy Murray OBE became the first British man in seventy-seven years to win the men's singles final at Wimbledon. He has been playing tennis since he was a boy and now, aged twenty-six years old, he has demonstrated his mastery of the game for the third time, following his win at the Olympics in 2012 and winning his first grand slam title at the US Open in 2013. Winning Wimbledon has completed the hat-trick. And this is just the beginning for a young man who is ranked No1 in Britain and No2 in the world in his field. That truly is mastery.

However, we don't have to win publicly to achieve mastery in our own lives. Beyond her neighbourhood reputation and now this book, Granny received no public accolades for her ingenious work – nor did she seek them.

What's curious is how the journey to becoming a master in any field begins. Does it begin with a vision of an intended future? Is it sparked by a passion? Is it fired by a desire to serve other people? Does it begin as a task that needs to be done and eventually becomes an unconditional love? Is it fuelled by appreciation from the people who benefit? Is it fed by the roar of the crowd? Is it kindled by the anticipation of a smile of joy on someone's face? Is it powered by an inner feeling of personal satisfaction?

The truth is that the inspirational catalyst for mastery differs for each of us and it doesn't matter what form it takes at all. The lesson from my grandmother's life of creativity suggests that the recipe for mastery calls for three ingredients: imagination, passion and perseverance – in whatever order you prefer.

Discover your treasure:

1. What resonates with you about this story?
2. Where in your life are you already a master of your craft? Is it in an aspect (or aspects) of your work or your personal life?
3. In which areas of your life would you like to move towards mastery? Be specific.
4. Why is it important for you to reach mastery in your chosen field?
5. How much time are you prepared to devote to your goal of mastery?
6. What would you be prepared to give up in your life so that you can reach mastery in your chosen field? For example, would you be prepared to give up watching TV, procrastinating or sleeping in late on weekends?
7. What do you imagine your life will be like when you have reached mastery?

8. HARNESSING TEAM SPIRIT

It was November, the time of year when the preparations for Christmas began with making Christmas cakes and puddings, as these needed several weeks to season before Christmas Day.

In Ireland in the 1970s, people didn't buy Christmas cakes and puddings in the supermarket. That would have been frowned upon since women prided themselves on their Christmas cake making prowess. Traditional Christmas cakes and puddings were regarded as luxuries, which people often made for each other as gifts. There was plenty of debate about what constituted perfection in the art. This involved a particular balance of moisture, fruit interspersed evenly through the cake and the 'right' amount of alcohol – a measure that varied widely. And the icing on the cake was just that: a bonnet of marzipan left to dry before a stunning white blanket was dolloped on top and then smoothed out, before being ornately decorated using a piping bag. It simply had to be right.

And so it was a Friday evening when my Mum unpacked the ingredients from her shopping bags. Flour, butter, sugar, eggs, mixed peel, glacé cherries and almonds were strewn around the kitchen table as four pairs of beady eyes looked on. Then she opened the cupboard and produced a bowl full of currants, raisins and sultanas that had been soaked in black tea for days. Granny had found a recipe in a newspaper which suggested that for the ultimately moist cake this practice of soaking the dried fruits in tea was a winner. Dry crumbly Christmas cakes and puddings were horrid in her opinion.

The greatest concern that my siblings and I had was to ensure that we would get to lick the raw cake mixture that remained on the cake beaters, spatula and bowl after the cake had gone into the oven. We had no interest in these rich fruity indulgences after they were cooked, whereas the anticipation of the creamy raw cake mixture ignited our zeal. We were high-spirited, giggling at nonsense and crowding around the kitchen table.

So there we were on that Friday night, about to embark on a complex mission with multiple tasks. Mum began to delegate the activities so that each of us could help. 'You, Mary, can chop up the glacé cherries,' she said. 'Claire, you can soak and peel the almonds and William can grate oranges and lemons.'

My little sister, Edel, who was born when I was six, was now two years old and as sweet as honey, with auburn hair and big blue eyes. She helped by tasting the raisins.

'Mary, when you have finished chopping the cherries I'd like you to prepare the baking tins for the cake and bowls for the puddings by lining them with grease-proof paper lightly covered in butter. We have to make sure that the cakes and puddings don't stick.' Mary agreed as she had almost finished chopping the cherries.

'When you have finished the almonds, Claire,' Mum continued, 'I'd like you to weigh the butter, sugar and flour carefully to the exact amounts in this recipe and put them into the mixing bowl. And when you have done the oranges and lemons, William, I'd like you to sift the flour into a bowl – slowly. Great, well done – everyone's doing a great job,' she told us.

And so the instructions went on all evening as we worked towards our purpose together. The kitchen was alive with industry and the sounds of excited chatter and laughter could be heard above the hum of the electric cake mixer. As we formed a busy team working towards a mutual goal, the connection created by our shared ambition and camaraderie was palpable. Hours later, the cakes were in the oven and the puddings, carefully covered with paper and tied up with string, were steaming in a pot of boiling water. The kitchen was filled with the aroma of baking, surely one of the most wonderful smells on earth.

As we had finished our cake making, it was time for our treat of licking the raw cake mixture from the cake bowl, the spatula, the spoons and the beaters from the electric cake mixer. I don't know what made raw cake mixture so utterly delicious to us, but we waited with bated breath for the moment when we'd get to lick the cooking utensils. My Mum wasn't pleased with our eating raw cake mixture, but she gave in and let us have it anyway. It was in the days before people were aware of the risk of salmonella from eating raw eggs – so don't try this at home!

Looking back, I realise the amazing power of our team as we united around a single goal and were directed by our Mum. Each of us played a fundamental part in making the delicious cakes and puddings. Although they weren't eaten for several weeks, our joy was in the connection, the opportunity to contribute, acknowledgement from our Mum and the reward of getting to lick the raw cake mixture. We had forgotten our competitiveness and given way instead to collaboration. There was a powerful synergy in the way that we worked together.

It seems bizarre that, today, such simple human needs as wishing to contribute in a meaningful way, to feel valued, connect joyfully with others and be rewarded fairly are regarded as luxuries in life. It seems to me that some people in society are able to eat up the whole cake while others don't even get to lick the spatula.

During my work as a consultant with many of the world's largest corporations, I'm often confronted by the turf wars that go on within these organisations. Often, the pressure to make money can end up eclipsing the deep sense of purpose with which the company was originally founded and the mission statement that it extols in its public communications.

But there are companies that operate differently. These are those in which the politics are minimised and everyone is engaged in the pursuit of mutual goals and committed to collaboration over competition – to 'we' over 'me'. I was heartened to watch a documentary about the story of Innocent Drinks. Their passion, innovation and teamwork are inspiring.

That day during our baking venture, my Mum harnessed the energy of four children under ten years of age to create an environment of connection, meaningful contribution and reward, without competition. Everyone had a task and there were no egos demanding attention or special treatment. Instead, there were industrious hands and minds focused on making a cake, with the gentlest guidance from her.

When our project was completed we celebrated together and revelled in the success of a mission accomplished. So at a tender age, I realised that I had already discovered three simple needs that make for great teamwork when they are met: the opportunity to contribute significantly, true connection with others and being acknowledged and rewarded for work well done.

Discover your treasure:
1. What resonates with you about this story?
2. Do you feel able to make a meaningful contribution in your work and in other areas of your life?
3. How well do you work in partnership with other people?
4. How easily do you trust and empower others?

5. How do you create the space for other people to bring their gifts?
6. What happens when you choose collaboration over competition?
7. How well do you feel you're being acknowledged and rewarded for your efforts?
8. How well are you acknowledging and rewarding others for theirs?

9. MANIFESTING CHRISTMAS

The excitement was almost unbearable as I lay in bed pretending to be asleep – or else Santa wouldn't come, I believed. 'At what time will he arrive at our house?' I wondered. 'Will we be first on his list or maybe he won't reach us until dawn? Will he bring what I asked for? Did my letter that was addressed to 'Santa, The North Pole' reach him in time? Did Mum remember to put it in the post, because I'd seen it in her handbag a whole week after I'd given it to her? I was full of anxious anticipation, such that my mind was perturbed by questions.

Then the words of a song popped into my head: 'He's gonna find out who's naughty or nice...' Was I naughty or nice? I realised that I'd been both, but I wasn't sure what Santa would think. I felt a pang of guilt and remorse for not being better.

When I look back on our family preparations for Christmas, it seems like such a big event. We spent weeks at school learning the story of the nativity – about the special baby born in a stable at Bethlehem and the three wise kings who followed a star to find Him, bearing gifts of gold, frankincense and myrrh. I had no idea what frankincense and myrrh were. 'They were strange presents to bring to a little baby – I would have brought a teddy bear or a rattle,' I mused.

We made decorations with crêpe paper in a rainbow of colours. We transformed toilet rolls by wrapping them in tinfoil into the celestial bodies of angels, with white paper doilies shaped to make their lacy wings. Our most unusual craft was making ornamental birds. We'd cut the bird shapes from cardboard and draw eyes on them with felt tip pens. Then we'd take feathers from an old hat brought to school by my Mum and glue the feathers onto our birds before sprinkling the birds with glitter and adding a gold thread to hang them on a Christmas tree.

Christmas cards arrived in the mail from the middle of December and every day bundles of them would flop through the letterbox. We each got excited when a card appeared with our name on it and we'd tear open the envelope enthusiastically.

In the middle of December our parents put our Christmas tree up in front of the window, so that it would light people on their way and show off our stylish fairy lights. On the branches, we hung coloured baubles, tinsel and fairy lights, and then the glittery birds that we'd made at school, before adding a star to the top of the tree. It was picture pretty once the fairy lights were switched on.

On Christmas Eve, the only thing that remained to do was leave a carrot in the living room for Santa's reindeer and a bottle of beer for Santa himself.

As I contemplated the journey we'd made in the run-up to Christmas I eventually lapsed into slumber, until I was awoken by William and Mary at the end of my bed, saying, 'Santa came and brought presents!'

'Have you seen the presents?' I asked.

My brother excitedly replied, 'Yes, you got great things.'

I ran into the living room eagerly. Our gifts were neatly stacked on chairs with our names on top. Wasn't Santa organised! I was so impressed that he knew my name and had written it neatly on my gifts.

I noticed an empty beer bottle and there was no sign of the carrot. 'Wow! Santa and his reindeer must have appreciated the beer and carrot, so it'd been worth leaving it out,' I thought.

Next, we went to wake our parents up and Dad groggily asked us the time. It was five twenty in the morning and Dad thought it was too early for us to be up. We didn't care! We animatedly told our parents what Santa had brought. My Mum sat up in bed and said, 'Oh my goodness, isn't that wonderful?' Dad chimed in with a few 'oh, greats' himself and we were all whispering vivaciously at five thirty in the morning about how wonderful and generous Santa had been.

I love this memory of Christmas because it was a magical journey of desire, anticipation and total trust that resulted in the manifestation of amazing presents. While I had the occasional pang of guilt that perhaps I hadn't been good enough, deep down I knew that Santa was a sure thing. I trusted that he was a benevolent character and I knew that the stories grown-ups told us about naughty children who only got a lump of coal for Christmas were untrue. They just said that to make us behave. Santa, I believed, was a kind and generous soul who wanted to make every child's heart sing.

Today, Santa is a great metaphor for manifesting from the Universe. I know that when I can harness those feelings of desire, anticipation and trust, something wonderful is well on the way to manifesting in my life. If, instead, I'm uncomfortable or frustrated then I know that either what I want is not true for me, or that I might not be ready to receive it or that it's time to let go. Often, letting go is enough to create the space for something to come into my life. At other times letting go is followed by moving on to pastures new.

So it's worth remembering how easily and innocently we could manifest our hearts' desire as children when we believed in dreams come true. We could easily tune into our hearts, set our intention by asking for what we wanted and then relax, trust and allow the Universe to do its magic. Today, we can still harness the same desire, anticipation and trust that we did as children on Christmas Eve. If we are drawn to what is true for us and we are ready to receive it, it will come to us. And if not, we can trust that the Universe has an even better plan for us.

Discover your treasure:

1. What resonates with you about this story?
2. If you believed in Father Christmas as a child, how did you feel on Christmas Eve? (If you didn't celebrate Christmas, think of another time of celebration and receiving gifts when you were a child.)
3. Recall that sense of desire, anticipation and trust that you would wake up and receive gifts.
4. Think about something that you desire now in your life: how do your feelings about it compare or differ to your 'Christmas Eve feelings' as a child?
5. If your feelings now are less positive, what stories are you telling yourself about your desire which might be getting in the way of your manifesting it?
6. Create a story about your desires that gets you closer to those childhood 'Christmas Eve feelings' of desire, anticipation and trust.
7. Let go of it the way that you did as a child when you eventually stopped thinking about 'Santa' and fell asleep until the break of a new day.

10. THANK YOU,
FLOWER SHOP LADY

Three lilies sit in clay pots upon my kitchen window sill. They flower several times a year when green stems snake their way up through their grass-like leaves and sprout clusters of tiny white flowers. They need little attention beyond occasional watering for them to thrive and bloom year after year. They began life as cuttings from a mother lily that Granny's mother presented to her when she got married. Granny's lily stood in a deep blue ceramic pot on the window sill in the house where I grew up. She told me the story of the plant and often said, 'Look after that lily when I'm gone.' Everyone knew that she prized it.

Granny was seventy-one when I was born and, as she had taken care of me as a pre-schooler, I had become close to her. Although I was aware that she was old, I wanted her to live forever and she promised me that she'd never die. Sometimes, I kept her company after school when the rest of the family went shopping. She was unable to cope with walking around shops – except at Christmas, when she braved the crowds and elements to ensure she had gifts for everyone.

When I arrived home from school on our special days together, I would be met at the door by the aroma of rhubarb pie baking in the oven. There was a bunch of rhubarb in the garden that grew every year and nobody could remember who'd planted it. It dutifully produced a host of ripe rhubarb stalks annually which Granny would use to make a delicious pie. As soon as the pie emerged from the oven, piping hot, Granny served us both a slice with a mug of sweet tea and we chomped away, licking our lips as the warm juice slipped down our throats.

One day, when I arrived home from school, Granny looked pale and was complaining of stomach pain. I was anxious because Granny was usually healthy. Over the next few days the pain didn't abate, so my Mum took her to the doctor. Diagnosis eluded the doctor and Granny was referred to hospital for tests. The house was empty without her and I felt lonely, but I'd visit her most evenings with my Mum. Granny was eventually moved to another hospital far away from us in Dublin for even more sophisticated tests. Now I saw her less often and her absence in the house was palpable.

The Mater hospital in Dublin was a grand old building on Eccles Street, a narrow lane with rows of red-brick terraced houses. Upon arriving, we climbed the wide stone steps to reach the majestic brown hospital doors. Once inside, we turned left and clip-clopped down the corridor and up the stairs to the ward to see Granny. Although she appeared frail, she seemed delighted to see us and I was thrilled to see her. I sat on the edge of her bed and we all talked for while.

Then I whispered to my Mum that I wanted to get some flowers for Granny and to ask the hospital radio to send her greetings. Having saved up my pocket money for weeks, I was especially keen to buy the flowers. I slipped away discreetly and clip-clopped back down the corridor, pausing only to write out the hospital radio request card and put it in the special box next to the entrance doors.

As I exited the hospital, I turned right and walked to the corner flower shop. It was alive with colour from the flowers in buckets around the shop. You could choose your own stems individually to make a unique bunch; however, in relation to my meager pocket money, they all seemed expensive. A display of sweet williams in various shades of pink caught my eye. 'Granny would love these,' I thought. Her beloved husband, the grandfather who had died before I was born, was called William and she often said that they were her favourite flowers. I bent down, selected three of the prettiest stems and took them to the counter.

The lady behind the counter accepted the flowers from me, asking, 'Who are these for?'

'My granny – she's in the Mater hospital,' I told her.

The lady looked at them curiously and then turned towards a bucket brimming with green stems and tiny white flowers. 'I think they would be nice with some gypsophila,' she said, adding two of these stems to my sweet williams. She showed the bunch to me and said, 'What about that?' I smiled and nodded. She wrapped them up and I was delighted that the price was just for the sweet williams because that's all the money I had.

'Thank you,' I said, before skipping back to the hospital with a happy heart and thinking, 'Granny will love these flowers.'

After making my way back up the stone steps, clip-clopping along the corridor and up the stairs to Granny's ward, I finally presented her with the flowers. Granny beamed with delight. 'Oh thank you, Claire,' she said. 'We'll ask for a vase to put them in.' I was thrilled.

On my future visits to see Granny, I returned to the flower shop and selected more beautiful stems for her. The flower shop lady added gypsophila when she thought it was needed and asked me to pay only for the flowers that I had chosen from the buckets. Proudly, I presented the bouquet to Granny and enjoyed watching her face light up.

On one particular visit, Granny looked especially frail. As usual, I went to the flower shop, but the lady who normally served me wasn't there. Somebody else was behind the counter. I selected the flowers and went to pay for them. The shop assistant was about to wrap them without any gypsophila. 'She must have forgotten,' I thought. So I said, 'Excuse me, what about the gypsophila?'

'Sure! Those are twenty pence per stem,' came the reply.

I had no more money so I said, 'Okay, I'll just have these please.'

The scanty bunch of flowers was wrapped for me and I paid the shop attendant. As I walked away I looked at the flimsy bouquet with disappointment. I was embarrassed to give these to Granny. 'What will she think?' I pondered with a heavy heart.

I continued walking slowly back to the hospital when suddenly I recognised a truth that changed everything: the original flower shop lady had given me a gift of the gypsophila which wasn't normally given free of charge. She didn't even know my name and yet she cared enough to ensure that the flowers I brought to Granny would delight her.

With a happier heart, I returned to the hospital and presented the flowers to Granny. She smiled warmly and said, 'Thank you, Claire; they're beautiful.'

Shortly after that, Granny passed away and went to join her own sweet William – in Heaven, I'm certain. As a family, we celebrated her eighty-three years on earth and shared our stories of how Granny had touched our lives.

Now, when I'm watering the three lilies on the window sill, I think about Granny and her kindness and generosity to everyone, especially her family. I also think about the flower shop lady and her random acts of kindness in creating beautiful bouquets of flowers for me to present to Granny. I never knew that lady's name, nor she mine. The flowers have long ago withered, but her generosity to me – a child, more than thirty-something years ago, wanting to give flowers to her granny – still lives on in my memory.

It is wonderful to know that anonymous, random acts of kindness can be remembered, thirty, forty, fifty years or more after the event. We're often being taken care of in ways that are beyond our awareness. Giving in this way to a stranger shows true generosity and the memory of this story compels me to say to you, Flower Shop Lady, wherever you are now, and to everyone who performs random acts of kindness – thank you from the bottom of my heart.

Discover your treasure:

1. What resonates with you about this story?
2. Can you connect now with some random-acts-of-kindness stories in your repertoire?
3. Can you recall a time when you realised that you were on the receiving end of anonymous generosity? How did it feel?
4. Begin to take note of how blessed you are by the generosity of other people on a daily basis: did anyone hold a door, hand you a tissue, carry your bag or offer you their seat recently?
5. Take the time to thank them in your mind now – gratitude is good for you.
6. See how it makes you feel when you go into your world noticing other people's random acts of kindness toward you or other people. It could make you feel better about the world we live in.
7. Look for opportunities to be generous towards others – both people you know and strangers – in simple ways that cost only a moment of your time.

11. HITCH YOUR WAGON TO A STAR

A sking unusual or challenging questions was my speciality as a child, and it drove my Mum nuts. One summer Sunday, when I was barely a teenager, was no different. I was walking alongside my Mum, enjoying the sunshine and the gentle breeze as she pushed my baby brother Tom in his pram. Tom was our youngest sibling, born when I was thirteen. He slept as my Mum and I chatted about school and contemplated the exams that were fortunately still a few years away for me.

'What essay did you write for your final English exam at school?' I asked her.

'It wouldn't make sense to you,' my Mum replied.

I persisted. 'Just tell me anyway,' I said.

And so she did. 'It was called "Hitch Your Wagon to a Star". Do you know what that means?' I had to confess I didn't. She told me that it was a quote from Ralph Waldo Emerson. Then our talk moved on to other things.

Yet the conversation stayed with me and, as an adult, I found myself wading through Emerson's work to find the source of the quote 'Hitch your wagon to a star'. Ralph Waldo Emerson was a nineteenth-century American lecturer, poet and essayist who believed in individualism, freedom and in nurturing a relationship with nature and the soul.

For many years, I believed that 'Hitch your wagon to a star' was about being visionary with ambitious goals. With that in mind, I wondered what my Mum might have written in her essay back in the 1950s. She became a teacher, wife and Mum to us five noisy, demanding children. I knew that she envisioned how her garden could be and spent time tending to her flowers, and coaxing my Dad to build rockeries so that she could grow shrubs and alpine plants. She had ambitions for how her children would turn out – perfect! We turned out to be imperfect humans doing our best, just like everyone else.

I wondered if she had had any wild dreams as an eighteen-year-old, writing that essay at school. It saddened me to think of the dearth of opportunities for women in the 1950s, compared to what we enjoy today. Perhaps she might have made different choices?

That was when I began to research Emerson's work and happened upon some interesting reviews of his writings. He believed that all things were connected to God and therefore divine, and that the truth could be experienced through nature. He championed the concept of individualism – self-reliance and the intrinsic worth of each person, who, he believed, could become corrupted by engaging with organised institutions. He led the Transcendentalist movement: a philosophy that believed in the inherent goodness of people and nature. Bemused, I realised that it didn't make sense that someone whose philosophy was about nature and the soul should propose a concept of indefatigable striving. It became apparent to me that he wasn't asserting this at all. Ralph Waldo Emerson's quote wasn't about unrelenting capitalism. It was about harnessing the power of the Universe, literally and philosophically:

> 'Unless above himself he can /Erect himself, how poor a thing is man!' but when his will leans on a principle, when he is the vehicle of ideas, he borrows their omnipotence. [...]Hitch your wagon to a star. [...]Work rather for those interests which the divinities honor and promote, — justice, love, freedom, knowledge, utility.

Ralph Waldo Emerson

I chuckled to myself, realising that I had misunderstood the phrase 'Hitch your wagon to a star'. Indeed, in Western society as a whole, we have been living as if we have collectively misconstrued Emerson's philosophy. In contrast, perhaps my Mum really had recognised what Emerson meant by that phrase. Everything she did seemed to be connected by a golden thread of principle – although this wasn't something she ever articulated, it was clear in her actions.

Recently, I heard that one of my mother's ex-students had said of her: 'She wasn't just a teacher to us; she was more like a mother.' It took my mind back to those bygone days at school.

Winters in the West of Ireland were often bitterly cold, the kind of cold that you feel through to your bones. The classroom was kept reasonably warm. However, my Mum was concerned to see that many children would drink cold milk or diluted juice concentrates at lunchtime. It bothered her and she felt that the children needed to be warmed up. But, each child brought his or her own packed lunch to school as there was no canteen or tuck shop.

She asked me one day, 'Do you think the children would like to have tea or hot chocolate at lunchtime?'

Since I was only seven, it felt like I had been consulted by the United Nations on world peace. 'Yes, I think they would like that,' I replied.

The next day, she asked the children to bring in a cup if they would like a warm drink at school and the following day several arrived, cup in hand. These cups lived in the school cupboard from then on and were used every day at lunchtime for warm drinks.

Like most teachers back then, my Mum had a camping stove on which to make her own tea. Every day, she boiled a kettle of water on the little stove and made warm drinks at lunchtime for all the children who wanted them. She was elated to see happy faces with pink cheeks and sparkling eyes peering over mugs of warm tea and hot chocolate.

Although making tea for the children didn't fit with my Mum's job description as a teacher, she didn't allow herself to be constrained by that. Imagine if we could all forget about job descriptions occasionally and act intuitively from the heart by noticing what else needs to be done to help the people around us. Wouldn't our world be different? Wouldn't it be more enchanting, joyful and nurturing?

That wasn't the only kindness that my Mum showed. There were many:

- she would tirelessly drive to visit my grandmother in hospital two hours away;
- she established the wonderful institution of Christmas cake-making in our home;
- she made up her own 'good food' recipes such as 'apple chunette' – her healthy version of apple pie;
- she would occasionally buy items that she didn't really need from a poor lady who needed the money.

The list is endless.

Whatever my mother understood by the Ralph Waldo Emerson quote I'll never know for sure. What is certain, however, is that people remember the way she touched their lives and not the goods and chattels that she collected along the way. She harnessed the omnipotence of the Universe because, even today, she is present in the minds of our family and of every child who was lucky enough to cross her path.

Emerson's philosophy is an interesting one to consider in a world in which we have found ourselves economically and morally at an abyss. It begs us to challenge our definition of success. Instead of the endless striving that has become increasingly ingrained in our society over the last thirty years, Emerson proposes a way of living that is guided by the Universe and that has respect for her resources and power. He suggests that we allow ourselves to be led by principles and ideas; and invites us to make it our goal to positively touch the lives of others and leave the world a better place than it was when we arrived.

> To laugh often and much, to win the respect of intelligent people and the affection of children… to leave the world a better place… to know even one life has breathed easier because you lived. This is to have succeeded.

Ralph Waldo Emerson

Discover your treasure:

1. What resonates with you about this story?
2. What does Ralph Waldo Emerson's 'hitch your wagon to a star' philosophy mean to you?
3. How does it relate to the way that you live your life?
4. How does it relate to your definition of success?
5. To what extent is your life led by your own principles and ideas versus cultural myths that you have unwittingly soaked up from society?
6. What other principles and ideas could you introduce into your life that would resonate better with you?
7. How would you like to contribute in a way that would serve other people and make the world a better place?

12. TOASTING THE PRIEST

Much has been written about the archetypal hero who sets out on a quest, travels to faraway lands, overcomes demons and dragons and eventually returns triumphant. As the least likely person to initiate such a mission, I was bewildered to find that, on my fourteenth birthday, my world was rocked in a way that shaped my future and set me on what I realised later was an archetypal hero's journey.

My family used to go to Mass on Sunday, like all Irish Catholic families did back in the 1970s and '80s. Chaos abounded in the house as all seven of us got ourselves attired for the weekly event. With reluctance, I'd don my Sunday best and shuffle to the car before my father drove the short distance to the church. By the time our family arrived, usually only minutes before Mass began, the choir would already be decimating the hymn 'Faith of Our Fathers'. Although enthusiastic, they were a harmonically challenged group in sore need of a choirmaster. God would, I'm sure, have appreciated their efforts.

Mass bored me – rambling sermons, stand up, kneel down, sit on the hard pew – it seemed pointless. The preacher was a canon – an elevated rank of the priesthood. A short, bald-headed man with beady eyes, he was well into his seventies. As he delivered the weekly sermon, he'd ramble inaudibly while rocking to and fro in the pulpit. Then his notorious little blue book would appear, in which was written the names of every family in the parish and the exact amount of their contribution to the Christmas and Easter collections, as well as any others. Shrugging his shoulders, he'd announce to the gratification or humiliation of each family their name and 'donation'. I glanced around on occasion to see the congregational response and noticed a mixture of smirks and pious faces. As shocked and bemused as others in the flock, I'm sure, I cynically thought, 'Shame and humiliation are great ways of stimulating generosity within the congregation.'

During the late 1970s, I was sent to boarding school with Mary. Our monthly weekend visit home afforded us a respite from the doctrine of role, rules and duties instilled by the Catholic sisters who ran the school. However, our return to school on the Sunday evening at the end of our weekend away was usually a fraught affair, as we got our month's supply of clothes and tuck bags ready.

Arriving back at school, we would alight from the car and cross the courtyard to enter through the double-doors, where we would be met by the intoxicating waft of musty building merged with stale cooking and the din of animated teenage chatter. Soon the school bell would clang and it would be time to go upstairs, make our beds and quieten down. Lights went out just before ten o'clock and we were expected to fall sleep instantly. In truth, we would creep under our duvet covers with torches and read our Mills and Boon classics or other dog-eared literature from a similar genre. These fantasy romance novels were passed from one hormonal teenage girl to another and were as close as most of us would get to a tall and swarthy suitor for many a year. Our avid undercover reading was punctuated with pop music from the pirate radio stations that we tuned into until we eventually fell asleep. Life rolled on like that until almost the end of my second year at the school.

It is a sunny May in 1980. School will soon be finished for summer, but before then I'll be celebrating my fourteenth birthday. 'I'd really like to go home for my birthday,' I tell my friends.

'Will your Mum come to see you?' they ask.

'I expect so,' I reply. Mum always visits us on our birthdays.

As my birthday dawns, I wake in bright spirits which are heightened when I receive cards and gifts from family and friends. After lunch, the birthday bumps tradition sees me flying in the air, screaming, and then laughing heartily as I recover my dignity once back to earth.

Mary is waiting for me at the end of the corridor. 'Claire, Dad is coming to take us home in the evening,' she tells me.

I am delighted: 'Hurray, I'm going home for my birthday after all!'

Then she says, 'Mum isn't well and so we're going home to look after the younger ones.'

'Mum's not well – what's the matter with her?' Fear grips the pit of my stomach. 'She's never unwell.'

My sister has no answer but explains that the message has come from one of the nuns.

A blur of worry mars the rest of my birthday. At seven-thirty in the evening Dad arrives with Auntie Nancy, my Mum's sister. 'Why is Auntie Nancy here?' I wonder. Now I'm even more concerned.

We get in the car and sit in virtual silence on the journey home. I break it occasionally to ask questions: 'Is Mum going to be okay?' But nobody answers me, beyond confirming that my Mum is in hospital. The car pulls up outside our house and we go inside. My three bewildered younger siblings greet us. At this stage William is aged twelve, Edel is eight years old and Tom is aged only fourteen months.

The phone rings incessantly all evening. Conversations are hushed. Auntie Nancy makes food but I can't face eating. I go to bed and toss and turn all night. Waking up, I find that the nightmare lingers. There's a dearth of information.

On my Mum's behalf, I go to church where it is First Communion Day for a class that she has been teaching at school. 'Someone from the family should be there,' Auntie Nancy has suggested and so, dutifully, I agree to attend. Yet people there keep asking me questions about my Mum that I simply can't answer. I feel foolish: it's as if they know more than I do. I walk home from church, hoping that I will wake up and discover that it's all been a horrible dream. But the day brings no better news of Mum's health.

I retire to bed for a second night of tossing and turning until eventually I fall asleep. I'm woken when someone enters the bedroom where Mary and I are sleeping. The clock shows that it's three in the morning. Two figures stand next to the bed – my father and aunt. 'Your Mum is really ill and she's going to be moved to a hospital in Dublin. We thought you might like to come now to see her,' I hear my aunt say. I'm only half awake. Then she adds, 'It might be the last time that you get to see your Mum.'

Grabbing the clothes that are lying at the end of my bed, I dress quickly – shaking all the while. Soon we're in the car on our way. We reach the hospital and are taken to intensive care where Mum is unconscious. I stifle back tears of utter devastation. Time passes and people move from Mum's room to the corridor and back again. Eventually, I'm alone with Mum. I talk to her, not knowing if she can hear me. It's not a time to release my inner chatterbox – there's only space to say what really matters.

'I love you!'

It's five am and I am waiting in the corridor, when I see my Uncle Jack approaching from the other end. My father and his brother haven't spoken for years, but now he's here to give his support. Why does it take something like this to make people realise what's important in life? Thank goodness he's here for my Dad.

At six o'clock in the morning, it's time for Mum to be taken to another hospital with better facilities. It's also time for us to say a sad farewell to her, but we remain hopeful – for a miracle.

We return home, tired yet wired. Dad goes to Dublin to be with Mum. Auntie Nancy takes care of us. It's another day of telephone craziness but there's no news – and so we want to hear news, especially good news. We want the miracle.

Day turns to night and back to day. On Monday afternoon the phone rings again and Auntie Nancy answers it. It's Dad calling from the hospital. There's a short conversation. She returns to the living room looking sombre. Quietly, she tells us, 'Mummy is gone.' The unthinkable has happened.

Grief hangs over us like a dark cloud. It is as if a malevolent force has wreaked havoc upon our lives, leaving us reeling in the aftershock. My emotions have frozen and only the adrenaline coursing through my veins reminds me that I am alive.

Dad returns and he tries to console us. Our house is buzzing with family, friends and neighbours who have come in sympathy. We get busy – making tea and sandwiches. It is cathartic buttering slices of bread, neatly placing slices of cooked meats on them and then chopping off the crusts. Thank God for visitors – the opportunity to focus on anyone or anything other than our broken-heartedness is welcome.

The following days were busy with preparations for Mum's funeral. The Mass was to be held in a sweet chapel in the parish where she taught, rather than the one with the raspy choir.

We arrived as a family to be met by a swarm of people, including many of her students and alumni who have come to pay their respects. Bouquets of irises and daffodils were everywhere, reflecting the season.

Decked out in their black frocks and white smocks, clergymen from several parishes paraded through the grounds. When I glanced in their direction I noticed the rambling old canon – a picture of virtue – thankfully not leading the Mass.

As soon as we stepped out of the car we were beset by people shaking our hands – and it felt intimidating. We were quiet and subdued, buoyed up just enough by the adrenaline of our shock to function normally. Dad held our baby brother, Tom, in his arms as we moved towards the church doors. The congregation of priests led the procession up the aisle and we followed, slipping into the pew directly behind them with our relatives behind us in turn. The old canon sat directly in front of me. Each priest had an unlit candle and I wondered, 'why?'

The occasion was fittingly solemn. The dulcet tones from a well-trained choir echoed from the gallery. Mass began. A priest who had known and worked with my Mum in the school for several years was leading the Mass and he choked back tears as he spoke.

It was time in the Mass to spread everlasting light. A giant Paschal candle was positioned at the front of the aisle. First lit at Easter time and then for Masses throughout the year, it symbolised resurrection and hope. The congregation stood as an altar server walked towards the Paschal candle and lit a taper from it. He went to the end of the front pew and began to light the candles of the priests. Reverently, he progressed along the row, lighting the candle of each priest in turn. 'Ah, now I understand the reason for the candles,' I thought.

Just then I spotted a tiny blue flame coming from the canon's sleeve. 'Oh my God, *the canon is on fire!*' I glanced around to see if anyone else had noticed. By now the flame was creeping up the sleeve of his smock. *The cannon was on fire!*

Then the priest sitting next to the canon turned, noticed and quickly grabbed a hymn book. 'What's he doing?' I wondered, stunned. 'It's not a time for hymns – is he planning to sing to the canon?' No, instead he began to beat the flames out of the canon's sleeve. Eventually the flames were quenched. Beyond a singed sleeve and a bruised ego, no harm had been done.

Yonder, the altar server was grappling to control his lit taper. Whenever he blew on it his breath acted like a bellows, fanning the flames. He scanned the room, but found nothing to help him. In a last ditch attempt, he threw the taper on the ground, leapt in the air like a lord in the carol and landed squarely on the taper, extinguishing the flame with a thud.

I was watching a farcical black comedy: 'Oh my God, my Mum would be mortified.' Yet it was funny and laughter began to emerge from inside me. And it wouldn't stop. I tried pleading with it as my body started to shake and it threatened to overwhelm me. After days of frozen emotions, it was the first green shoot to signal the end of the ice age. The blissful release of tension, fear, grief, loss and emptiness was welcome. Yet it was coupled with guilt: 'Laughing on this day is wrong – I must be crazy or bad,' I worried. Suddenly, my thoughts were confirmed as I felt someone poke my back from the pew behind as if it to say, 'Claire, you must behave!'

Looking back, I can see now that the laughter was a gift. It was the first time in days that I had felt any emotion at all. Humour took me over in that moment and it busted the sinister cloud for a while and melted the numbness. Doom and gloom didn't honour my Mum or celebrate her life. She wouldn't have wanted us to be sad, although it was difficult not to be.

The world I lived in had changed forever. It was the beginning of a chapter of dark days and nights for me, in which there were many false dawns before enlightenment. It called for me to dig deep into my own personal resources and to reach out to others for help too. I didn't know then what I know now: that in the midst of dark clouds, the light is waiting to burst through when we're ready to embrace it again.

Discover your treasure:

1. What resonates with you about this story?
2. What factors have influenced your path in life?
3. How do you feel about the gift of humour in your life?
4. In what ways do you use it to bring more lightness into your life?
5. How do you feel about letting go of sadness, guilt and other negative feelings, and allowing yourself to be happy when you are ready?
6. What help and support have you received from others?
7. What have you learned about yourself and others?
8. What new, more empowering story can you tell about yourself?

13. BLESS HER WOOLLEN SOCKS

My return to boarding school in September 1980 brought relief from the profound sense of emptiness that permeated our house. It is extraordinary how loudly desolation can make its presence felt. With my home life offering a constant reminder of the gaping loss in our family, boarding school seemed the lesser of two evils. It offered me a means to escape and the chance to forget by getting involved in the world of school, especially as it was going to be an exam year for me.

Yet this return to boarding school was so different to those times when my Mum had prepared everything and I'd simply packed my suitcase. She would send us back with new clothes and bags of goodies to sustain us; although I had taken it for granted at the time, I now realised how loved and cared for I had been. Dad tried to make everything better but nothing he could do relieved the bleak and inescapable winter that raged inside me.

There was, moreover, little warmth and loving kindness at the Catholic boarding school where I was about to commence my third year. Sadly, these were the precise qualities which were most lacking in my life. At school, 'perfect order' was expected, which was in sharp contrast to the chaos I felt inside. The nuns weren't unkind but they were task-orientated. I didn't blame them, as they had to manage over ninety hormonal boarders, as well as an additional three hundred day-girls. All the same, the fact that I understood their challenge didn't make it any easier for me to be there.

All too soon I was back at boarding school and becoming reacquainted with my old friends. I hadn't seen them since May as most of us lived far away from each other. I quickly discovered that there was little comfort to be gained from sharing my feelings of sadness with them; the few attempts I made were met with quietness and a subtle change of subject. 'It's too scary for them to contemplate what's happened in my life,' I thought, 'and they don't know how to respond anyway.'

From that first day back, I learned to put on a brave face and engage in chit-chat, wanting the girls to believe that I was okay and mostly trying to convince myself that I was just fine: 'Now which dormitory am I sleeping in? Where is my book-shelf? Which shoe room am I supposed to be using?' Conversing with the girls and dealing with practicalities that first evening focused my mind until it was time for us to go upstairs, make up our beds and get a good night's sleep before we began the new term.

We woke to the familiar bell clanging and the nun on duty stomping around the dormitory, ensuring that everyone was awake and out of bed. The usual drill ensued – getting washed and dressed, breakfast in the dining hall, collecting our books for school and walking to that term's new classroom.

As I wandered to class with a friend, we stopped briefly to scan the school notice board where timetables and lists of teachers and class prefects were displayed. 'You're Class Prefect,' my friend said.

'Me, really? You're joking!'

'No, look – your name's here.'

I was surprised. 'Have they made a mistake?' I thought.

The Head Mistress, Sister Patricius, was walking by and greeted us both.

'I notice that I'm Class Prefect?' I said.

By now a group had collected around the notice board. 'Yes!' she said, looking at me intently. Then she addressed the other girls: 'There is a great deal of depth to this young lady, more than I ever realised.' In that moment I felt seen and acknowledged in a way that boosted my self-esteem.

As we all filtered away to our classes, the daily routine was once again established and the new school year was underway. Later, in a quiet moment, I pondered the comment that Sister Patricius had made and recalled a letter that she had written to me during the summer with a message of sympathy and hope. I had been deeply touched to receive it and responded with a note in which I had explained my heartfelt sense that: 'my Mum is still with me.'

'Was she referring to my response to her letter?' I wondered. 'What had she thought before – that I was a ditzy thirteen year old?' She'd have been right – I'd been exactly that until a freight train had knocked down the world that I'd known, changing it irrevocably. Business as usual wasn't an option: I had to navigate in fog to find the way.

At boarding school, our contact with the outside world came through phone calls and letters – and so it was always good to be reminded that people hadn't forgotten about us. There was one pay phone in the school, which usually had a queue of girls waiting to use it. Occasionally, when it was unused during study time, the phone could be heard ringing with an inbound call and someone would slip out from the study hall to answer it.

One such call was for me and so I went to the phone. 'Hello.'

Dulcet tones responded, 'How are you, Claire? It's Auntie Vera.' Auntie Vera was one of my Mum's four sisters. She was a fun-loving lady, the tallest of my Mum's family and had their characteristic good looks. Her kind voice was comforting. Knowing she was busy with four children of her own, I was moved and delighted that she'd called me.

We chatted on for a while. 'Is the food good and are you eating properly?' she asked. 'Are you warm enough?' – always a good question when you live in the West of Ireland with the biting winds from the Atlantic coast sweeping their way inland.

By the time we said our goodbyes I felt heartened. Afterwards, I thought, 'She's asked me the kinds of things that Mums ask.' Mothers feel your cold, your hunger and your pain as well as your joy, your happiness and your enthusiasm – which is part of the pain and the ecstasy of being a mother.

A week later, I was having lunch in the dining hall on a regular Wednesday. The menu was shepherd's pie followed by sticky currant buns, which we were buttering as our mail was delivered to us. I was feeling indifferent about the mail, having no expectations, when to my surprise I was handed a package. After I'd wiped my hands, I took the brown, padded bag that had my name and school address written on it in blue ink and which had layers of brown tape sealing the ends. It felt soft and squidgy. I wondered what was inside. 'Go on, open it,' I heard around the table. Placing my fingers under the tape, I deftly ripped the package open. Inside there was a layer of tissue paper, which I peeled away quickly. Now I could see two pairs of winter socks. The top pair was rust-coloured, thick and woolly. Underneath was a second pair – chunky in beige with brown spots.

'Who has sent me these beautiful socks?' I wondered.

A small envelope lay beneath them. I tore it open to reveal a sweet card: 'With love from Auntie Vera.' My heart leapt – 'Oh wow!' I hugged the socks to my face, charmed by them. Those questions my Auntie had asked me on the phone were not random platitudes. She cared enough to send me a thoughtful gift. I decided to wear one of the pairs the following day.

And so I did. Indeed, I wore and washed both pairs until they became threadbare. In addition to being toasty warm, those magic socks had been sent to me with loving intention.

The practical wisdom from this story is that if you live in or are planning to visit the West of Ireland, you need a darn good pair of socks to keep your feet warm! And there is a deeper message too. When you're in a dark place in your life and somebody reaches out to you – it's a miracle. You're in bleak and foggy territory and you're not even sure if there is a brighter place. And even if there is, you don't know how you're ever going to make it there - you are simply putting one woolly foot in front of the other to feel your way forward. You need human angels to lighten your step. They can't travel your journey but they can support you on your way. This will sometimes take the form of a kind word or their giving you an opportunity to be involved and feel good about yourself, as happened when I was made Class Prefect. At other times, their support can be more direct – reaching out to you to enquire about how you are doing, sending you a card and – if you're really lucky – sending you pairs of magic socks.

There are opportunities every day in our lives to give and to acknowledge receiving – be it a kind word, a card, the gift of our time or something specific – practical or whimsical. If we become more mindful of how others have reached out to us when we've needed it and if we notice in turn where we could extend ourselves to help our friends, we will open up our lives to enchantment. After all, giving and receiving are what make our world go around – these acts create the reciprocal flow of energy between people that nourishes our souls.

Discover your treasure:

1. What resonates with you about this story?
2. Which people have been your angels on your life's journey?
3. Consider who in your life has touched your heart and take the time to thank them individually in your heart now – or even in person.
4. Consider who in your world you could reach out to with your help. This could be somebody that you work with or in your personal life.
5. What does that person need that you could give them – a kind word, standing up for them, your time and attention, or some practical help?
6. Decide what action you are going to take and follow through on it.
7. Once you have done it, reflect on how your actions have enhanced your life and theirs.

14. MINDFUL GOALS

The creaking of the stairs and the feeling of trepidation return to me whenever I recall that 'midnight feast' at three o'clock in the morning at boarding school.

Several months into term, the monotony of our boarding school routine was setting in. Every day, we were scheduled to within an inch of our lives by bells and orders that had to be followed. As we were never allowed to go beyond the school grounds, we were confined to the school campus. The mere presence of a male on site, unless he was a teacher or maintenance man, catalysed the nuns into calling the local garda station to have him removed. My urge to break free from the chains of control was palpable. But I was Class Prefect and expected to uphold the rules and show leadership – to be a good girl, just like when I was the teacher's child at junior school.

My avid reading of Enid Blyton's books about the antics of teenage girls at Malory Towers and St Clare's boarding schools had versed me in the art of creating midnight feasts. I had gained first-hand experience too, since each dormitory held an annual midnight feast, organised by the older girls. And so it became my ambition to organise the best midnight feast ever, to which I invited three of my closest friends, who were equally enthused by the mission.

Our first dilemma was: 'How do we get access to good midnight feast fodder when we're not allowed to leave the school grounds?' We each had pocket money for the school tuck-shop, but the shop only sold sweets and ice cream and wasn't stocked with midnight feast provisions. We wanted more substantial grub such as sandwiches, cake and biscuits – that's what constituted a great midnight feast.

We chatted about our mission with day-girl friends in our classes. To our delight, they offered to help us. We set about writing a shopping list of foods that appealed to everyone's tastes, then pooled our money and passed the list and the loot to our co-conspirators. Their enthusiasm for our venture was impressive even though they would be at home, tucked up in their beds, while we feasted in the dead of night.

Two days later, our helpers showed us the fruits of their labour when we got to class. We were flabbergasted. True to what we had requested, they had bought our favourite cakes, biscuits and cold drinks. But they had gone way beyond the agreement and had even made sandwiches for us, which were neatly tucked into a lined biscuit tin. They also surprised us with a homemade chocolate-biscuit cake, which had been made especially for us. Squeals of thank-you from us showed our appreciation for their generosity.

A glitch in our plan then appeared, because we hadn't considered where we would store the food. Putting our heads together, we explored the options and agreed to spread the booty around between the four of us. We stashed it in desks, cupboards and lockers. That way, if one location got rumbled by the nuns, the impact on our mission would be minimised.

At last it was the evening of the big night. We drifted off to our dormitories with the saintliest demeanours we could muster, while hiding our naughty secret and feeling smug. We had our wake-up plan in place and were going to meet at three o'clock in the gym.

At two forty-five in the morning my friend woke me. Blinking with tiredness, I could hardly open my eyes. Then I remembered why I was awake – it was time for the best midnight feast ever! I dragged myself out of bed and reached around in the dark for my torch. Then, putting on my dressing gown and slippers, I slid out between the curtains of my cubicle. My friend and I walked gingerly along the corridor of the dormitory, past the room where Sister Clare, the nun who was head of the boarding school, slept. We were relieved to have made it over the first hurdle by reaching the landing by the stairs.

The first step on the stairs creaked much more loudly than the dormitory floor that we had just traversed. The noise was eerie in the old building. We braved the second step and then the third with my heart thumping as if it were going to jump out of my chest.

'Is that a door opening?'

'Shssh!'

'Maybe the building is haunted?' we whispered to each other.

The dark of night and the creaky building were catalysts for our paranoia. We shivered and kept going. When we reached the bottom of the stairs, we looked at each other and giggled, releasing the fear that we'd carried down the stairs. We scuttled like mice across the corridor to the new wing, where we retrieved our stash of food on the way to our destination in the gym.

There was a chink of light under the gym doors. We glanced at each other for support, gulped and gently pushed the doors open. Phew! Our two comrades were there already. We all began to laugh, muffling our mouths so that no sound could escape.

It proved to be a delicate task to tear away the wrappers and open tins as noiselessly as possible. Once the food was unwrapped and arranged, it made for an impressive spread. Eventually, we sat campfire-style around our feast and raised our fizzy drinks in plastic cups to congratulate ourselves on our coup. It was time to eat. 'Does anyone feel hungry?' There were tuna and egg sandwiches, cakes and biscuits and even the dream chocolate-biscuit cake waiting to be eaten.

It was a quarter-past three in the morning and I had been willingly jolted awake from a deep sleep. Adrenaline was coursing through my veins and my body was in fight or flight mode, as if I had just outrun a wild boar. An appetite for even the most indulgent fare eluded me. Taking a sandwich and biting into it, I found that, while it was tasty, I felt like I was force-feeding myself. We were not out of the woods – the gym lights could have been switched on at any moment, signalling that we had been rumbled. The usual punishment for this sort of misdemeanour was to lose out on break time for several weeks by being made to help with clearing and washing-up after dinner. 'If we get discovered in the gym having a party in the middle of the night we might be washing dishes forever,' flashed across my mind.

I ate a little more; otherwise the mission would have seemed such a waste. The others were feeling a similar loss of appetite, combined with nervousness. Soon we drew our meal to a close, but not before acknowledging that we had accomplished our mission to create the best midnight feast that we'd ever experienced. Then we put everything away and shuffled back to our beds to catch some sleep before the bell started clanging in the morning.

The following day, as I thought back on the feast, I felt a sense of achievement and disappointment at the same time. Yes, we had achieved our goal but it hadn't brought us real pleasure. The anticipation and planning of the midnight feast had been more exciting than the activity itself. The feast had originated from our desire to escape the monotony of boarding school life and to create some excitement. It had achieved a 'high' for us temporarily, but it hadn't brought us any true and lasting pleasure. The goal had proved meaningless, although we'd mustered the courage to pursue it.

When I think about the way our world works today, I recognise the same mindless pursuit of what we believe will be the best feast ever. We want more of whatever it is that we believe will rescue us from a life of meaninglessness. We compete with others and live on the edge as if we're being chased by wild boar. These goals are little more than mirages in the desert, which bring us temporary highs but often lack the soul nourishment we crave.

We need to stop and ask ourselves what is the reason behind our goals. We need to ensure that they are aligned with our highest values and that they will bring us what we're really seeking. We need to differentiate for ourselves between our true goals and those that are mindless indulgences or are motivated by our desire to keep up with social pressure. That's not to say that there's no place for indulgence – it can be a welcome release. However, it's important to recognise when we're chasing a temporary high, so that we're not disappointed to discover that it lacks the nourishment and sustainability we can get from the pursuit of other goals, which would bring real meaning to our lives.

Discover your treasure:
1. What resonates with you about this story?
2. Consider something that you want now in your life: where does that desire come from – your own heart or from social pressure and others' beliefs?

3. What story are you telling yourself about what you believe your goal will bring you, once you have it? (Money, happiness, fame, love, peace, sense of achievement, etc…?)

4. Now ask yourself why these things are important to you?

5. Then ask yourself what challenges you'll have to overcome to get it? (Financial, hassle, risk of rejection, uncertainty, fear of failure, etc…)

6. Are the benefits of the goal worth the investment of your time, energy and emotions?

7. Is it a meaningful goal that will nourish and sustain you? If not, do you intend to pursue it anyway or perhaps choose a story that feels more right for you?

15. RUDDERLESS

L ife at home had changed dramatically without my Mum and with only my father looking after us. He never got over his loss. The feminine balance that my Mum brought to their partnership was noticeably absent. His moods were often low.

Immediately following the loss of our Mum, my father had been concerned about who would take care of our baby brother, Tom. One morning, I arrived at breakfast to find that Mary, Auntie Nancy and Dad were already up. They told me – each adding a sentence or two – that the plan was for Mary to take a year out of school to look after Tom all day and then Edel too when she got home from her classes in the afternoon. The following year I would be expected to do the same.

I was quiet and not sure how to respond. I didn't feel like I had much choice in the matter. While I understood the dilemma, I wasn't convinced that it was the ideal solution and I hadn't been involved in the discussion to explore the options. However, the thought of saying 'No!' or even 'I'm not sure that I want to do that' brought up feelings of guilt – so I reluctantly went along with the plan. My sister duly spent a year taking care of our younger siblings and now, following my exams, it was my turn to do the same.

Like any kid, I was secretly smug that school was 'out' for a whole year – like the longest summer holidays you can imagine. No more early rising, no more uniforms, no more rules for twelve months. However, to a fifteen year old, school is life: it's about friends, it's about growing up, it's structure, it's mind-expanding; it's a sense of achievement and identity. Without that network of support, there would be a chasm in my life. I worried about how a year away from education might affect me: 'Will I forget much of what I've learnt and how easy will it be for me to pick up school again the following year?' I was sad when I thought about my friends and classmates progressing to the next year and leaving me behind.

After all her efforts to ensure that her children were well educated, my Mum would not have been pleased to see me being taken out of school. As a teacher and a Mum, she placed a high value on our learning and development. If we ever had to take time out from our classes with the occasional cold or flu, she was always concerned that we were missing out on learning.

So September came and there I was, at home every day. Mornings were a rush of hustle and bustle as William, now aged thirteen, and Edel, now aged nine, got ready for school. By nine o'clock, the house would be empty except for me and my toddler brother, Tom, who was two-and-a-half years old. He was an adorable child with light brown, springy curls like Little Lord Fauntleroy; his hair was theoretically 'too long', but nobody wanted to cut his locks. He'd look at me with his irresistible big brown eyes, framed by sweeping eyelashes, and his sweet button nose and use self-created words to ask for what he wanted. In particular, he used words with a never-ending 'ing' for emphasis when he had an impatient request that needed to be met immediately, such as 'I'm hungeringeringeringeringering' or 'I'm cold, put on my cardinggeninggeninggening.' And, in the morning, I'd make baby porridge that he called *booley*, his interpretation of a brand name that was too complicated to pronounce for a toddler who liked to ask for what he wanted. Tom ate, played and napped, and then repeated the cycle again.

As is typical for autumn in Ireland, the weather was often overcast and cloudy although not yet cold. The kitchen in our house was a big, square family room with a white table surrounded by red chairs. The heavy chairs made a scraping noise when you pulled them away from the table – I remember that it drove my Mum crazy. 'Do you have to drag the chairs across the floor like that?' she'd say.

An old transistor radio on the sideboard was switched on from breakfast until dinner, daily. My father would listen to the news several times a day. He'd come back to the house at lunchtime to eat and tune in to the broadcast; 'Sssh!' he'd demand at the slightest sound as he listened to the day's atrocities.

'Why does anyone want to listen to all that depressing news that drags your spirits down?' I often thought. As soon as the news was finished, I'd tune the radio to a music station to boost the atmosphere again.

Conversation with my father was difficult. For a long as I could remember, he had always been a great storyteller who could keep people entertained for hours with his tales. However, his stories became darker after he lost his wife. No amount of sharing them seemed to bring him catharsis.

Initially, I tried to keep the house straight, mundane as I found the task. But nobody ever said, 'Thank you,' leaving me feeling unappreciated; and soon it became as soul-destroying as it was dull. Just a few months earlier, my mind had been engaged in learning, exams, drama, yoga, debating and organising midnight feasts. Now I was alone on a farm in the middle of the Irish countryside, with no access to anywhere and my friends an hour's drive away in boarding school, as the hours, days, weeks and months stretched out before me.

My new life was unstructured, the complete antithesis of boarding school. Having never had to structure my own time, I didn't really know how to do so effectively. All that unstructured time is not healthy, especially for a fifteen-year-old teenager. As the months of isolation and loneliness dragged on, I found that I was rudderless in an ocean with no sign of land in any direction.

As I surfed the waves of everyone else's needs, I began to create structure in the only way I knew how at the time – by controlling my food. Initially, I oscillated between binging and starving, feeling a heady sense of control when I was able to abstain from food for days, followed by self-loathing when I binged afterwards. Despite knowing that my behaviour was crazy and unhealthy, I found it hard to break the cycle of guilt for eating followed by the penance I decided that I needed to undergo to assuage it.

However, there were fun times when Mary was home from boarding school. We'd go out together with old friends from primary school. On one of these occasions we celebrated the results of the exams I'd taken in June, before leaving school for the year. Another time, during the October half term, we found ourselves in conversation with a group of friends after an evening of dancing. Amongst them was a cute guy who attracted my attention. I was drawn to his playful spirit and twinkling eyes. We flirted subtly. It was fun. Then it was time for Mary and me to go home. But during the long days of November and December that followed, the guy kept popping into my mind. 'How cool it would be if he was my boyfriend,' I thought. I wondered if I'd see him again, especially as my social life was so sporadic.

Christmas was challenging. Despite Dad's efforts to make it enjoyable for us, there was always a gap without Mum. I had regained some sense of balance in my eating habits, although my relationship with food was still dysfunctional.

On New Year's Eve, Mary and I had an opportunity to go out and socialise at a nightclub that accepted teenagers. My father drove us into town eight miles away. As we approached the doors of the venue, the hits of 1981 were booming out: 'Every Little Thing She Does is Magic' by The Police, 'Don't You Want Me' by The Human League and 'Stand and Deliver' by Adam and the Ants. I was buzzing, thrilled to be soaking up the high spirits of the evening – in dramatic contrast to those long winter nights at home. Dancing made me feel so vibrant and alive.

About an hour later, the DJ decided to slow down the music and play a smooching set – cueing the guys to ask the girls to dance and my escape to the ladies room. I didn't have a boyfriend or know many boys, and so I was loath to appear as if I was waiting for a knight in shining armour to approach me. Upon my return, the slow set was still playing. 'Hopefully it'll finish soon and then I can dance again,' I thought. At that moment, there was a tap on my shoulder and I swung around.

Standing before me smiling was the cute guy from the half term night out. 'Would you like to dance?' he asked, taking my hand and leading me to the dance floor. Soon we were dancing to 'The Land of Make Believe' by Bucks Fizz.

James and I spent the rest of the evening together before his friend drove us home.

'So when can I see you again?' James asked.

Much as I wanted to arrange a date I had no idea when I'd get to go out again. 'I'm not sure,' I said, hoping not to ruin the moment. 'It's not often that I'm allowed to go to nightclubs.'

James wasn't going to accept such a vague answer. 'Okay, so I'll call you,' he said, 'and then, whenever you're able to go out again, let me know.'

It was a deal and he took my home phone number, promising to call me the following week. True to his word, he did.

My New Year's resolution was to improve my eating habits. 'I'll eat regular meals like a normal person,' I thought. This became relatively easy for me now that I had a different kind of relationship to focus on beyond the one I had with food. It worked well for a while until I gradually found myself reducing the quantities at each meal until they became so small that I was continually losing weight.

Counting calories became an obsession for me once I discovered the tons of health and slimming magazines and calorie-counting books that my Mum had stored under the cushions on the sofa. 'No wonder she was so slim,' I thought. Within weeks I had memorised the calories of most of the foods listed in the book. As each day broke, I would begin planning what I would eat, when I would eat it and exactly how many calories I would allow myself. I feared that without this kind of control my weight would spiral out of control. The reality that I was unhealthily thin didn't stop me.

Gradually, I was shrinking physically and emotionally. Soon I was so tiny that I felt like a child, not like an adult, and most of all I wanted somebody to take care of me. I wanted to have fun with my friends, like most fifteen year olds do. People noticed that I was disappearing. They heard my call but they didn't understand it. Instead they focused on fixing what they saw as the problem: 'Claire, you're too thin – why don't you eat? You don't look well.'

Meanwhile, James called me every Friday evening, which was the highlight of my boring week. I looked forward to seeing him again.

'What will I wear when I do go out?' I thought. Although I had some nice clothes, there wasn't a great variety among them. Like Cinderella, I wondered what I'd wear to the ball – all I needed was a Fairy Godmother.

One day, as I wandered down the hallway at home, I spotted Granny's old Singer sewing machine in the room where she used to work. I went into the room, dragged a chair over and took a seat behind it. As I moved the wheel forwards and backwards, and pressed on the foot peddle, I decided: 'I'll make clothes like Granny did – how hard can it be?' I looked around. 'But what will I make them from?' I had no teenage fashion patterns, nor any fabric. 'I know,' I decided, 'I'll excavate the cupboards and find garments that I can remodel. There may even be some oddments of fabric from Granny's dressmaking days.'

The wardrobes and kitchen cupboard yielded the best results. As well as old clothes in need of remodelling, I found some unused cotton fabric – a blue and a white piece. The sewing-machine drawer had plenty of cotton thread in basic colours such as black, white, red and blue, as well as needles and pins and Granny's canister of oil.

There wasn't much fabric and I wondered what to make with it. 'I'll make a sleeveless mini-dress with a dropped waist, white on top with a blue skirt,' I eventually decided. I set to work with Granny's old dressmaking scissors, cutting out the shapes for the top and the bottom. It wasn't going to be Haute Couture, but for a skinny fifteen year old it didn't need to be. It took me a couple of days to stitch the bodice and skirt seams up and then join them together to make the dress, before finishing off the neckline, shoulders and hem. '*Voilà*, I will go to the ball!' I thought as I danced in my bare feet before the mirror, pleased with my creation.

Then I stopped. 'I would love new shoes to wear with it,' I thought. When my Dad took me shopping soon afterwards, I asked if I could have some new shoes. I didn't often ask for anything because I knew that Dad didn't have much money now that he was the sole breadwinner. He agreed. As I wandered around the shops my eyes fell upon a pair of dainty gold shoes with kitten heels. Gold shoes were all the rage. These were perfect and soon they were mine.

When my sister and I went out for Valentine's weekend celebrations in February, I had the chance to wear the blue-and-white mini-dress with the gold shoes. I spent the evening with James again and we had a lovely time. He gave me my first ever Valentine's card, which boosted my self-esteem.

Yet I felt different to everyone else, because they were at school with their friends during the week while I was at home babysitting. I was now painfully shy with little sense of control over my life. However, something had shifted – I had connected with my own creativity, resourcefulness and style, and somebody was showing an interest in me.

The dressmaking that I had learnt from Granny became a hobby. The calorie counting became less obsessive and I gained enough weight to be reasonably healthy. James continued to phone me every Friday for a while and I saw him a few more times. Then, like many light-hearted teenage relationships, it ended that April at Easter time as quickly as it had begun.

However, it was spring and the schools were moving into their final term. Soon it would be summer holiday time. The weather transformed from the coldest January for fifty years to one of Ireland's sunniest summers. And in September I would be returning to school, shaped by the year that I had spent learning to find my own rudder in an ocean of time and space.

We all have times in our lives when we are rudderless and uncertainty abounds. The predictability of a life in which every moment is scheduled is never desirable and yet, while the opposite may seem appealing, it can be equally disconcerting. What is most difficult about being rudderless – especially when we feel we haven't chosen the situation for ourselves – is that we are left feeling powerless; whereas when we have opted for uncertainty we can call it an adventure. Today, the concept of a gap year either between school and university, or immediately after university, has been growing in popularity. It is a self-selected rudderless state in which people are attracted by the adventure that the unknown promises. But it's not for everybody – it depends on our own personal barometer for certainty and uncertainty.

Sometimes, when we have stability in some areas of our lives, we are able to cope well with instability in others. For example, if our work and relationship are stable we may cope better with the upheaval of moving home. If we're settled at home and with our partner, our perspective on redundancy may be brighter than if we were alone. However, when we have uncertainty in several core areas of our lives and we believe that this isn't our choice, it's easy to feel victimised and resentful because we imagine ourselves to be powerless – although, in truth, we are infinitely powerful.

Unfortunately, being rudderless is not a rare situation – it's a reality of our world today. It concerns me to see how our global economic crisis and shifts in technology have cast so many people into uncertainty. How to find a sense of sanity when we're feeling rudderless has become a pertinent question for many of us. Often we're angry simply because we feel that something has been imposed upon us. We all feel so much more valued when we're genuinely invited to collaborate in the way forward. That, of course, doesn't always happen and may not even be feasible.

So, when we find that we're adrift, the only way to accept and even embrace the situation is to take a different perspective. With time, we might even come to see our altered circumstances as an opportunity for adventure –

although at first this perspective might seem like a step too far. We may need time to accept the situation and own our feelings about it.

It might be easier to take more of a 'big picture' or even a spiritual view that it's all happening for a purpose. We don't always know why something happens but a belief in a benevolent purposeful Universe can offer us a calming mindset. We can ask: 'What does the Universe want for me now? What resources am I being called upon to develop within myself?' It could be that we need to make a stand and say, 'This is not the truth for me'; or that we connect with our inner resourcefulness and find a way through the challenges before us.

It is heartening to remember that we humans are unstoppable wave-surfers with infinite imaginations. From time to time, we may have to dive below the surface to find our treasure and our challenge may be the catalyst that enables us to go deeper, embrace the next step and become the person that we're meant to be.

Discover your treasure:
1. What resonates with you about this story?
2. Have you been feeling rudderless in any area of your life (through redundancy, leaving school or university, ending a relationship, starting a business or any other uncertain circumstances that can create a feeling of being lost)?
3. What opportunities for a new story or even a new chapter might there be in this situation for you?

4. How is it pushing you beyond your comfort zone?
5. What personal resources do you need to draw upon?
6. Who can help to lighten the load and brighten the road for you?
7. What would be your ideal outcome in this story – can you turn it into your best chapter yet?

16. GETTING INTO THE FLOW

The most feisty and independent woman I know is my Auntie Chris. When I was a child she lived in London and visited Ireland at Christmas, Easter and during the summer. Perennially glamorous, she looked fabulous in whatever she wore. In addition to glitzy accessories such as silk scarves and jewellery, and her stylish sense of colours and shapes, she had a perceptible *je ne sais quoi*.

Her trips to Ireland became more frequent and lengthy after we lost our Mum. Auntie Chris was my father's sister and when she visited Ireland she stayed with his brother, my Uncle Jack, in the house where my Dad's family had grown up. Her visits filled us with excitement because she could engage with our teenage passion for trendy clothes. Incredibly generous, she brought us gifts of high-fashion gear from London that we cherished.

At Christmas, she would arrive with beautifully wrapped gifts. Amongst them were jackets, skirts and brightly coloured sweaters that she'd knitted herself. Her whirlwind of energy lit up our house and she introduced us to foods that were regarded as exotic in the West of Ireland during the 1980s, such as curry and chilli con carne. At Christmas, she made chestnut stuffing.

Chris would often borrow Uncle Jack's red VW Beetle, which he had owned for what seemed like forever and take us out shopping or visiting friends. One of those days was particularly memorable. We had planned to go shopping with Sister Canice, my father's aunt. Small, round and devoutly religious, Sister Canice was in her sixties.

And so the day began. Chris, Mary and I got into Uncle Jack's red VW Beetle, which would always splutter before the engine would start. We made our way to the convent that was Sister Canice's abode. A nun since leaving school, she emerged from the convent dressed from head to foot in black. It was a hot day and I wondered how she could stand the heat in that outfit.

'Hello,' she said chirpily, 'how are you, isn't it a lovely day?' – all run together in the one sentence.

'Hello, good, yes it's lovely,' we responded in unison.

Sister Canice perched like a duchess in the front seat of the car, her purse on her lap. As Chris drove away from the old convent building, my Great Aunt made the sign of the cross beside her and said, 'Please God, we'll have a safe journey!' And so we were on our way.

Soon Chris was driving along the roads as fast as the old Beetle could muster. As the leafy trees and green fields flew by, Sister Canice sighed and said, 'Thank God, we're on our way now!'

It was a glorious summer's day, with a clear blue sky and the sun shining brightly. The shadows from the leaf-laden trees dappled the grey road as the sunlight peeped through the boughs. I could feel the warm sun on my arms through the car window. Sister Canice gasped with wonder and exclaimed, 'Glory be to God, it's a beautiful day!'

In spite of the cars speeding by on the opposite side of the road, a few impetuous drivers overtook us. Chris rattled on in the indefatigable old Beetle, working it as hard as she could. A woman on a mission, she was focussed, with her head poking forward towards the windscreen. Sister Canice remarked, 'Thank the Lord, we're nearly there!'

We reached the outskirts of town, which was busy with the hustle and bustle of market-day people and traffic. Chris drove around looking for a parking space, remarking with frustration, 'The world and his wife are in town today!' Up one street and down the next, soon she was driving around in circles to the point of distraction, the gears crunching and the hand break creaking as she navigated through the traffic to find that elusive parking bay. With her hands clasped in prayer, Sister Canice said, 'Please God, we'll find a space soon!'

Then Chris spotted a space between two parked cars, which she decided was hers. She accelerated forward and indicated as she began to reverse. Oops, was the space going to be a bit of a squeeze? Forward again and then, with a marathon of manoeuvring, she finally managed to park neatly. With that, she stopped the engine and swiftly pulled on the hand break. Sister Canice blessed herself and declared, 'Thanks be to God!'

Quick as lightning, Chris shot her a glance and corrected what she believed was Sister Canice's misplaced gratitude: 'It's not thanks be to God,' she said, 'it's thanks be to *me*!'

As a teenager observing the scene, I was amused to watch the friendly spat between these two ladies. However, as I recall it now, it raises a question about whether success in any area of our lives is the result of our efforts or the gift of a Higher Power – the Universe, God or some other deity. Can we afford to sit back and do nothing, or do we have to make an effort to reap the rewards from our actions?

There is a saying that: 'God helps those who help themselves.'

Similarly, the Indian sage Patanjali said: 'When you are inspired by some great purpose… your mind transcends limitations, your consciousness expands in every direction… Dormant forces, faculties and talents become alive.' These words suggest that we're at our best when we're in partnership with the Universe, whereby we're in the driving seat yet there is somebody sitting beside us, helping us to read and interpret the map.

To my mind, there is a behavioural continuum from wilful action to naïve waiting – or, in other words, from a place where we believe that we have to do it all, to a place where we believe it'll all be done for us, like magic.

Wilful action can be a bit like trudging on through life disregarding the signs. Yet, simply because wilful action implies we're taking responsibility for ourselves, it probably has a higher chance of yielding success for us than merely waiting naïvely for something to happen magically. So we do need to take *some* action.

That said, an element of waiting and trusting is important too. Composer Claude Debussy said: 'Great music is about the space between the notes.' In life, it's likewise good to wait, listen and then act mindfully, ultimately creating a healthy balance of action and inaction. We can move forward and at the same time respond to the feedback that comes to us from our world in the form of signs, hunches, feelings or comments from other people.

So, to get back to these two lovely ladies, Chris and Sister Canice, on that sunny market day in town – what might have seemed like an unlikely travelling and parking partnership was in fact a perfect combination of effort and trust, action and inaction – and a great lesson it was too for me.

Discover your treasure:
1. What resonates with you about this story?
2. Think about the life story that you want to craft for yourself.
3. Have you got a good balance of activity and inactivity – planting seeds and letting them grow?
4. Notice when your effort becomes too much and you move into tension and stress – it's time to create space.

5. Notice when you might have been contemplating and waiting for too long: do you need to move into action?
6. Do you feel centred and aligned with the story that you want to create?

17. THE CRUSH

Having spent a year at home, I couldn't face the idea of going back to boarding school where my old friends would have moved on a year without me. So in September 1982 I went to a school in the local town.

It was a naïve choice in that I had no idea how difficult the change would be for me. Instead of the short walk along the corridor from the dining hall to the classroom that I'd been used to when boarding, I faced an eight-mile bus journey to school – and the bus stop was more than a mile walk from our house along dark, unlit country roads, through which I had to make my way in all sorts of weather.

The first day, dressed in my new navy uniform and blue duffle coat, I walked to the end of our road with William to meet the school bus. The bus arrived and to my dismay it was a rattling contraption with cold hard seats. I could hardly hear myself think above the din of noisy kids, who ranged in age from twelve to eighteen. Some of the younger ones were as giddy as goats and chewed smelly bubble gum. I said, 'Hi,' and then smiled and sat on an uncomfortable seat, thinking, 'Oh my God, what am I doing here?' The bus took over an hour to reach its destination as it travelled up hill and down dale to collect children from the various parishes whose youngsters attended the school.

Shy, skinny and always cold, I was different to the more confident girl I'd been when boarding fifteen months earlier. Upon arriving at my new school, I went to see the deputy head, Mrs Hussey, as I'd been instructed. Another girl was waiting outside her office. 'Is she new too?' I wondered.

Mrs Hussey duly emerged, wearing a neat two piece suit, her jet black hair stiff with hairspray. She peered over her horn rimmed glasses and spoke to us in a loud matter of fact tone: 'Right, you two are in class 501 up the stairs. I'll take you there.'

She marched down the corridor ahead of us. The lesson had already started when we entered the classroom and the other students stared at us as if two camels had just walked into the room. I found the attention disconcerting and wanted to disappear through the floor. We were shown to desks next to each other and we sat down as the lesson continued.

At break time, the girls crowded around us and quickly established that the other new girl came from a small town which was home to a group of boys they liked and where there was a regular youth disco. The girl knew several of these boys well and was an immediate hit with our classmates – everyone's new best friend.

In contrast, I felt trapped inside my shy, lost self. Where I'd once been a confident girl who loved drama, debating, writing essays and organising midnight feasts, I could barely string two words together without feeling awkward. I really wanted to fit in, especially with those girls who seemed to be having the most fun. Yet, during the first two months, I felt invisible at best, certainly not popular and usually not wanted. On top of this, the weather was harsh, making the journey to school difficult to handle. My hands and feet had chilblains and I couldn't get warm. By October, life felt bleak and hopeless and I regretted moving schools.

In November, the girls decided to go to see Chris de Burgh in concert in Dublin. 'If I can go too,' I thought, 'I'll get to know them better and they might realise that I'm nice.' So I invited myself along and bought a ticket from the girl who was organising the trip.

The concert day came and a group of us, girls and boys, caught the train to Dublin. Sitting together on the train was conducive to good conversation and, as we reached Connolly Station, I felt that I was beginning to make some connections. The concert was magical and everyone was in high spirits. Afterwards, we walked five miles across Dublin to the house in which we were staying that night, where we arrived exhausted at one o'clock in the morning. We spent the following day roaming around Dublin until we were ready to take the evening train home.

That weekend marked the first significant step I made in making friends with these girls and boys, although there was still a long way to go before I would feel that I belonged in their tribe. However, things became easier as I began to be more accepted by them and started going out socially with them.

Romance was never far from the conversation as teenage romances and breakups flourished. Since the brief relationship I'd had during my year at home, I had been a single sixteen year old. There had been one other boy besides James who had caught my attention. I had met him a year earlier as we both stood outside a disco. He spoke to me and I turned to see a tall, remarkably handsome and charming guy. I found myself tongue-tied, blushing like a schoolgirl – which was ironic because I didn't actually go to school that year. He went to the boy's school next to my new school. Now I was hoping to meet him socially and make a good impression. 'Perhaps he thought that I didn't like him or that I was snooty or stand-offish,' I worried, and I was determined to show him that wasn't true about me.

I soon realised that this particular beau was on the wish list of several other girls and that he already had a girlfriend. But relationships at the ages of sixteen and seventeen never lasted very long and so I wasn't deterred. With a typical teenage mindset, I thought: 'If I can go out with Mr Popular it means that I'm acceptable, worthy and likable. I decided to bide my time. Meanwhile, I wouldn't consider going out with anyone else. Patiently I waited, believing that my life would be transformed when our romance finally happened.

However, we hadn't met socially since that awkward moment a year earlier. A friend had asked him if he 'liked me' and she told me that he'd said yes and confirmed that he was in a relationship with somebody else. When I heard that, I glowed, secretly thinking 'I knew it!'. I was certain it was only a matter of time until he would be mine.

Sometimes I'd see him across the road at lunchtime and my heart would leap. One day, he began to walk across the road to speak with one of my friends and I could feel my heart beating faster. Quickly I thought, 'It's my chance to show him how wonderfully charming, enchanting, intelligent and witty I am.' Before I knew it, he was standing opposite me on the other side of the street railings speaking to our group. He glanced at me and said, 'Hi-ya.'

By now the charming, witting, intelligent idealised self-image that had occupied my imagination only moments before had disappeared, and in her place was a blushing, bashful, babbling wreck. 'Hi,' I said back and that was the extent of the conversation. 'Gosh Claire, profound,' I thought afterwards, 'that was so different to the last time you spoke (or didn't speak) with him. Damn, damn, it wasn't supposed to be like that!' I felt ashamed. 'That shy person isn't really me. Next time I'll make a good impression,' I decided.

School wasn't enjoyable. I felt so off centre after my year at home that even my writing muse seemed to have abandoned me. School essay writing didn't engage me in the way it used to. The motivation to sit down and pick up a pen eluded me and my inspiration seemed to be hidden in a locked cupboard with a lost key.

Eventually the summer holidays came. School was out, the weather was sunny and there was a disco to celebrate. Absolutely everyone from the crowd who normally went to discos was going.

Then the memorable day arrives. It's the night of the disco and I spend ages getting ready. Perfect clothes and hair are essential so that I can feel good about myself. As I arrive with my friends the music is pounding the song 'Sweet Dreams' by the Eurythmics and Annie Lennox's operatic rock tones resonate through the hall.

After engaging in some animated chatter outside the hall we go inside. Almost immediately I spot the object of my affections and I feel my heart flutter. Standing there in his leather jacket, he looks like the character Danny Zuko from the movie *Grease*, hanging out with his male friends, no girlfriend in sight. 'Wow, he's single – it's now or never – how exciting!' The music is blaring, the disco lights are dazzling and I am dancing blissfully with my friends.

One hour into the evening I hear the DJ say, 'Okay folks, we're going to slow things down a bit now.' Cue the slow set. Everyone clears the floor to make space for the couples. It's an opportunity for the guys to ask the girls to dance and I'm sitting there with my heart racing, hoping that tonight will be the beginning of a new romance. 'Oh my God, how will I feel if he asks me to dance?' I wonder. He glances in my direction and my heart somersaults. He's walking towards me. 'Don't look presumptuous,' I tell myself. 'Be cool and feign surprise when he asks you to dance.' By now I'm shaking. 'Relax,' I hear myself say.

He is a metre away from me, walking like a man on a mission. Two more steps and he bends down and stretching out his hand - he asks the girl sitting next to me to dance. She gets up straightaway and walks to the dance floor with him, where they dance closely for the whole slow set.

I sit motionless, frozen to the spot, my heart beating wildly. I feel foolish. 'After all those months I've invested, waiting patiently, he just walked up and asked my friend to dance – and while she was sitting right next to me!' I fume. And there she is, dancing with 'my guy'. I'm broken-hearted and furious with myself for being so naïve. I don't know where to look; I feel silly. 'Everybody knows I fancied him – what must they be thinking?' I take a sharp intake of breath and swallow my shame.

Soon the slow set comes to an end and my friend walks away from the guy. She's not interested in him – she likes somebody else. I stand up, shrug off my discomfort and go to join the rest of the group.

It's time to dance to the loud music. It's time for me to move on gracefully. That's exactly what I'll do.

Then I realise that I am absolutely fine without this guy in my life. During all those months that I waited patiently for him to become my knight in shining armour, I have made friends. I have established myself within the tribe. I belong! I didn't need to be propped up by anybody else's popularity. I am my own person – and that's all I need to be.

When I first started to look back as an adult on my naïve teenage passion, I began to wonder why it's commonly called a crush. Is it because it requires you to crush your own magic and greatness and then project these qualities entirely on to someone else? You put someone on a pedestal and you look up admiringly at them from a place where you have diminished yourself through your low self-esteem. You trick yourself into believing that you need the false god that you are idolising to rescue you, in order for you to be redeemed and feel whole again. You have crushed yourself and then you unwittingly crush the other person with your neediness – and so naturally they run for the hills.

The perfect circumstances in which this kind of crush could flourish were created by my low self-esteem, as I tried to fit into a new school and a new social environment. I wanted to belong to a tribe like most teenagers do – and indeed everyone does. That desire to belong is what underlies the power of many great brands, be they in fashion, music or what we drink. Paradoxically, we love our individuality and yet we want to have a sense of belonging, too – it is a basic need for us as humans.

I also wanted somebody to rescue me and give me the sort of attention and validation that I really needed to be giving to myself – but I just didn't know how to do that then or, indeed, until several years later.

Now, I look back and I feel compassion for myself – as I do for you if you have fallen into the same trap of worshipping what I call 'false gods' and giving your power away, rather than nurturing your wonderful, charming, magical and witty self. Whenever you don't keep clear boundaries and limits, you create the possibility to be untrue to yourself in order to win the validation of other people. Any relationship – whether work, love, friendship or family – has the potential to become unbalanced if we become untrue to ourselves in an attempt to win the approval of others.

So stay centred and ask yourself whether what you're doing feels true, or whether it feels like you're valuing somebody's approval so much that you're not taking care of your own needs. And give your enchanting self the attention, love and support that it needs to bloom!

There is a sweet spot where wonderful connections are made when we value our selves completely and we also totally respect each other. Find it within yourself and all your relationships will be better for it.

Discover your treasure:
1. What resonates with you about this story?
2. Think about the relationships in your life – friends, lovers, work and family – and identify how equal you feel in each significant relationship.
3. Now identify places where:
- You give your power away – you feel inferior, intimidated, awkward and separate.
- You usurp other people's power – you feel superior, smarter, judgemental, pitying, self-important and separate.

- You own your own power and you empower others – you feel a sense of mutual respect, compassion, love, caring and connection
4. What new stories can you tell yourself to create a greater sense of equality and connection in all of your relationships?
5. How can you negotiate healthy boundaries and limits to create a good balance of giving and receiving in your relationships, knowing when to make more effort and when to walk away?
6. Tune into that place in you where you know what's going on in any relationship and find that sweet spot where you value your own worth and respect the value of others too.

18. THE GRADUATION

It was summer of 1984, exams were over and school was finished for good. A new life beckoned, although I had no idea where it would take me. As Sean Covey describes the state of many teenagers in his book *The Seven Habits of Highly Effective Teens*, 'I had no plan and no plan to make a plan.' In the year that I left school, Ireland was in deep recession with few prospects for youngsters, including those with university degrees, and people were emigrating in droves to search for work. 'Will the last person to leave Ireland please turn the lights out?' was often said in jest, but it was far from funny and too close to the reality that many of us were facing.

So the preparations for my graduation dance were as far into the future as my thoughts stretched. All the girls were planning to wear posh frocks and make-up and to be escorted by a gorgeous guy. So I was excited but also in turmoil. Firstly, I didn't have a posh frock to wear. There wasn't a great deal of money to spare at home, what with Dad having five kids to care for, and so I didn't want to ask for something as whimsical as a graduation dress – although I'm sure he would have bought one for me if I had asked. Secondly, who should I invite to the graduation dance as my partner? It needed to be someone I'd like to spend the evening with, naturally. I also wanted to avoid the small-town gossip that might ensue if I invited somebody local and they said 'no thanks', in which case my fragile ego would crumble. Finally, I wanted to throw a party at home after the graduation, which would be the icing on the cake. My Dad agreed to my bringing friends home after the graduation and I decided I would organise the party myself.

I eventually decided to invite a guy who I'd met several months earlier at a nightclub. It had happened when my friend Hilary and I had been studying chemistry together all day and felt we deserved to go out and have some fun. The evening had promised to be just another regular night, meeting up with other friends and laughing and dancing. However, we'd been at the club for only a short while when a young, dark-haired guy with the biggest smile ever had asked me to dance. We danced for a while, but when I was about to slip back to my friends he smiled and said, 'Aw, just one more dance;' so we danced some more and before I knew it with his gentle persuasion we had spent the entire evening dancing together. He told me where he lived and it was far away from me. He explained that he was spending the weekend with his cousins and so I didn't expect to see him again.

Hilary suggested that I invite the dark-haired guy to be my graduation escort. When I protested that I didn't have his phone number, she arranged to get it from a friend of his cousins. With the telephone number in my hand, I had no excuse not to make the call. Since I hadn't seen him for months, I was nervous when I rang him. Our conversation was brief but his answer was yes, so I had overcome one of the hurdles to going to the ball: I had a Prince Charming to escort me.

There was still the question of that dress. What would I wear? Could I design and make my own dress? Having already made dresses and skirts for myself, I had discovered the joy of reincarnating a garment into a new persona, as I'd seen Granny do. 'There is that scarlet skirt I've hardly worn,' I thought. 'And I have a few metres of black cotton fabric lying about in the cupboard that could be useful.' The idea came to me to create a dress with a double-layered skirt and a black bodice. The underskirt would be black, while the top skirt would be red and hitched up at the front to make a tulip shape, revealing the black skirt beneath.

I set to work with enthusiasm on creating my design. I made good progress at first but soon reached a plateau, as I was unsure how to hitch up the red skirt over the black one neatly. I turned my attention instead to getting the house ready for the party, as well as organising the event. The graduation was nearing, leaving me little time in which to make everything happen. I did my best to prepare – there was so much to do but soon there were only three more days to go.

When I talked to my friend Emma about my progress, she asked if I'd like her help with the dress. She was a talented dressmaker and a creative soul who I knew I could trust with my design. Gratefully, I gave it to her and she promised that it would be ready the day before the graduation.

I continued preparing for the party but discovered there was so much to do that I plateaued there too. Fortunately, Mary came home for the weekend from teacher-training college and brought two friends with her. They promised to help with the party. 'What a relief!' I thought.

The day before my graduation dance, I went to collect my dress from Emma's house. She brought it out on a hanger to show me and it was beyond my wildest dreams. She had created a sweet bow to hitch up the red skirt over the black underskirt, making a beautiful upside-down tulip shape. I loved it.

The day of the graduation dance arrives and so do my sister and her friends. 'You just get ready for your grad,' she encourages me, 'and we'll organise the party.' So I do just that.

Dressed for the occasion in the tulip frock, red beads and shoes with red bows, I get into the car with Dad, who drives me to town and drops me at Hilary's house where I have arranged to meet her. I'm planning to meet my graduation escort later at a hotel. 'Will I even recognise this guy?' I worry to myself. It is a year since I've seen him.

Hilary and I walk together to the hotel and once inside the bar I glance around, but I can't see my graduation escort anywhere. 'Oh God, don't say he hasn't turned up! Hilary, he's not here,' I cry. I'm bewildered. She nudges me and indicates close to where we were standing. 'What?' I say.

'Sssh, he's over there, sitting on the bar stool.'

I look where she's pointing and there is a tall guy wearing a suit and tie, sitting on a stool. 'Him?' I wonder.

'Yes, that's him.'

'Really?'

'Yes!'

I have my doubts: he has his back to us, so how can Hilary be sure? I approach the guy and immediately he swings around. 'Hi!' we say in unison. It is the right person, but he is taller and broader than the boy I had met a year earlier. We chat for a while as Hilary meets up with her own beau for the evening.

Then we all set off to the graduation dance. As we approach the venue, it is alive with music and *joie de vivre*; several graduation couples are milling around outside. We go inside and settle with the rest of our group at a table towards the back of the room, where we enjoy an evening of good food, dancing, fun and more alcohol than is ideal.

We are driven back to my house, several miles out of town, for the party that I'm holding. I'm not sure what to expect since my sister has taken control of the arrangements. As I walk into the house I am stunned. She and her friends have created a fabulous party atmosphere with decorations and music; and they have prepared the most wonderful spread of food, much of which has been brought along by the guests and other dishes that they have created from scratch during the evening.

I discover that my graduation partner is a keen singer and guitar player who entertains us all for hours, playing and singing until morning. It turns out to be a tremendous party – beyond my wildest dreams.

I look back with delight at my graduation evening which was a success despite my initial concerns. What made that happen were the collaborative efforts of the people who stepped in to help me: Hilary, Emma, Mary and her friends, Dad, who let us hold the party, and the guy who became my escort were the key players. The other friends who came to my party and brought food for the spread were essential to the evening too.

The truth is that we can accomplish little on our own. Even when it's our vision, we need the support of other individuals to help us execute it. When we consider people whom we regard as amongst the most successful in the world, business leaders, presidents, celebrities – all of them have a network of people who have supported their success. We're all creating our own individual life stories and at the same time we can empower each other's success stories too. Our lives are intertwined in such a way that as we serve others by becoming valued members of the supporting cast of their life script, we are in turn empowered to become the star in our own life script.

Discover your treasure:

1. What resonates with you about this story?
2. What new story or chapter do you want to create in your life right now?
3. Are there people who might be able to help you bring this new story to life?
4. Do you trust and value the gifts that they have to offer?
5. Can you let go of control and open up to integrate the gifts and talents from these people that may be different to yours?
6. How can you create the opportunity for these people to engage and help you now?
7. How is your life story intertwined with those of others and what gifts in the form of opportunities, passions, talents, experiences and resources do you exchange to empower each other?

19. BECOMING THE SCRIPTWRITER

I finished school with no great plan for the future. Although I had applied to university none of the courses I had earmarked appealed to me enough to invest three years in studying them. I was adrift. Like many Irish folk, I found myself moving to the UK. It was my Auntie Chris's idea – she seemed to think the move might offer me the direction I needed. She lived in an apartment on Holland Park Avenue, close to Notting Hill (since made famous by the movie of that name).

'What was I going to do in London?' I wondered. Work and study, she suggested. My top priority was to earn some money and so I scoured the recruitment agencies and the newspapers to find work. 'What experience do you have?' was the mantra of every company, but at eighteen years old I had none so my search wasn't easy.

As I was flicking through the local paper, an advertisement for an administrator at a bespoke tailoring company in

Savile Row caught my eye. I called and within minutes I had secured an interview for the following day. When I pushed through the glass doors into the old fashioned shop with its panelled walls and polished wooden tables displaying men's accessories, I was confronted with a row of suited, middle-aged men as starchy as the shirt collars on their shop displays. It seemed both an intriguing and intimidating place to be; one where everybody called each other Mr or Mrs. I felt as if I'd been transported to the set of the TV comedy series *Are You Being Served?*

I was ushered into a small, old-fashioned office where I was interviewed by the manager and shown the plethora of seemingly mindless tasks that I'd be asked to do. There were no computers and so good hand writing was essential – 'I can manage that,' I thought.

'Can you type?' the manager asked.

'He's discovered my Achilles' heel – think fast,' I fretted inwardly. I babbled something about learning quickly and practising on my Aunt's typewriter. Mindless as the activities sounded, I wanted to earn money and therefore – as long as the work was legal, honest and decent – I was prepared to do it. I waited with bated breath as I watched the manager thinking.

'You'd really brighten the place up around here,' he said.

I looked around at the regiment of old boys on the shop floor and thought, 'I know what you mean.'

The manager pondered some more and then said that he would let me know later whether I had got the job. No sooner had I returned to the apartment than the phone rang and he offered me the job. I was delighted and I accepted it gratefully.

I started at the tailoring company the following week and also signed up to study maths in the evening at a local college. This was my Aunt's idea too but since I was drifting in life at that stage I went along with it, although frankly it would have been hard to find a subject that I enjoyed less. I already had qualifications in mathematics from school and, despite my lack of direction, I knew that more trigonometry or calculus would not enhance my life.

Soon I moved out of my Aunt's apartment into a student hostel in a nineteenth century mansion in Notting Hill Gate, where luckily I got one of the few private rooms. Run by Irish Catholic nuns and with breakfast served from seven to nine o'clock every morning, it was a bit like being at boarding school again but with fewer rules.

After ten months at the tailoring company, I went to work for the loans division of a bank. Banking was regarded as a respectable profession in those days and my family was impressed that I was working there. Meanwhile, everything about the job jarred with me.

One Sunday, as I'm wandering around Kensington High Street, immersed in the buzz of cosmopolitan London, I bump into a man who's walking from a restaurant towards a waiting taxi. He stops and speaks to me: 'Are you American?'

'No, I'm Irish.'

'Hey, so am I!' he replies, and he asks if I'd like to go out for a drink with him. For some strange reason – probably because of the Irish connection – I say yes to a complete stranger. We arrange to meet later that day at Jimmy's Wine Bar on Kensington Church Street.

It's fun to go out with somebody, although I soon realise that he and I have little in common. He is several years older than me, passionate about music, a rocker dressed in drainpipe jeans and a leather jacket, with longish, dark, curly hair. He plays guitar and hangs out with people who desperately want to become celebrities. We date for a while, but our differences soon seem insurmountable and create conflict between us – so the relationship gradually begins to wind down.

Meanwhile, I endure life at the bank, regularly asking myself, 'What am I doing here?' It is made more intolerable because I have started to wake up each morning with a feeling of nausea that continues for most of the day. 'Oh God, hopefully I'm not pregnant,' I think, and do a test.

I wait for the results with bated breath: 'Oh no, I am.'

I sit motionless, thinking, 'What now?' Is it worth telling this man? I decide to tell him anyway and he is less than thrilled.

I share my plight with two Irish friends at the hostel who are working in London for the summer. The parents of one of the girls are visiting London. Her Mum being a general practitioner and her father a lawyer, she thinks they might be able to offer some practical wisdom. They are kind people and encourage me to tell the Mother Superior at the hostel and my father. Mother Superior proves to be gentle and wise.

I am not entirely convinced about telling my father, but I go along with the suggestion anyway. When I do tell him, with the best of intentions he begins to suggest solutions that are not acceptable to me. I know in my heart that it is absolutely true for me to bring my child into the world and take care of it myself, which makes this a non-negotiable situation from my perspective. This marks a turning point for me: the decision that is right for me and my child are all that matter even though I'm breaking the ultimate Irish Catholic taboo of having a child out of wedlock. I cannot afford to go along with somebody else's plan and live with the consequences of it for the rest of my life.

The space for personal choice was limited in large Irish families like ours. Because of this, I would typically either go along with a plan and feel resentful, or rebel against it and feel guilty. I didn't have the detached assertiveness that comes with the confidence that it's acceptable to negotiate. Behave, be quiet, do what you're told, don't make waves – this was the way that children were raised in the 1970s, which is a far cry from the dizzying amount of choice that children are afforded in the twenty-first century, western world.

The direction that I choose creates conflict between my father and me. He attempts to convince me that I'm making a choice that will prove difficult. He is right – I am – but when it comes to their children, mothers don't scare easily. And the best choice in life isn't always the easiest one. That conflict unfortunately marks the beginning of several years of virtual silence between us.

Meanwhile, dragging myself into the bank every day, I eventually tell the HR manager why I've taken a couple of days off sick. I've been finding it hard to stay upright, let alone work all day. That same afternoon, I am told that the bank wants to end my contract. The truth is that they are doing me a favour and I am relieved to get away from there, it's so not me.

During the next few months, I wake early and spend hours wandering around Kensington Gardens, Hyde Park and Kensington High Street. I receive wonderful letters from people that keep my spirits up – especially those from my father's youngest sister, Auntie Betty in California, who has two teenage sons and is separated from her husband. 'I know you'll be a wonderful Mum, Claire,' she writes. Her belief in me is precious. She and my Uncle Jack, who is also my godfather, send me gifts of money, which is thoughtful and kind of them.

I go into labour on the very day that my baby is due and, after twelve hours of my getting euphoric and spaced out on gas and air, Ryan is born the following morning at St Mary's Hospital in Paddington. He looks bewildered by the bright lights and people. The nurses check him over and then wrap him up and put him in my arms. His father arrives and says, 'He's lovely.' Ryan is a miracle and we can't stop looking at him.

After that, his father came to the hospital every day and seemed completely mesmerised with Ryan. 'This is what it's all about,' he said.

'What do you mean?' I asked.

'Families, kids – it's what life is about,' he replied.

Ryan's father asked me to move in with him. Thinking it would be a better option than going back to a hostel and to goodness knows where from there, I went along with the idea. When I left St Mary's Hospital, we collected my things and Ryan and I went to live with him in his apartment near Notting Hill. I took care of Ryan while his father worked. Eventually I went back to work too, taking on temporary, part-time projects that I enjoyed, working with an organisation that aimed to inform and protect consumers.

However, by now I had a burning desire to go to university and build a career for myself. Through Ryan's father I met several people who were pursuing their ambitions to become celebrities – whether by modelling, singing or acting – although most of them were waiting tables in restaurants or such like while, ironically, they waited to be noticed, hoping for their big break. It was a bizarre world – easy to see why people got hooked on the adrenaline rush of a fantasy that seemed to manifest for only a few.

Wanting a career path that seemed more realistic than that, I applied to study Business and Finance and was accepted and started the course when Ryan was eighteen months old. With that step, I began to feel empowered. I was becoming the scriptwriter of my own life.

When you have no plan in life, this can create the space for somebody else to identify a path for you. Nature abhors a vacuum. Hence you find that all kinds of ideas come your way, which can be wonderful or a nightmare, depending on whether you feel that you're being empowered or allowing yourself to be fixed by others.

Yet nobody can fix, reject or even empower you without your permission. You have to be complicit in the process. It is only if you accept what is coming your way that it can affect you. However, sometimes we can be passively complicit – going along blindly, naïvely trusting that somebody else's plan for us is automatically in our best interest. Regardless of their good intentions, it might not be right for us.

That's why it is so important for us to create our own connection to the Universe, to tap into our muse and make decisions that are congruent with our own values. But this doesn't mean that it's not important to listen to other people's ideas and feedback. Listening to others can expand our thinking and help us to discover solutions co-creatively that are even more perfect than those we might have arrived at alone. The key is to listen out for what resonates with us positively or negatively. We know when something resonates positively because, metaphorically speaking, it switches an energetic light on for us. We can integrate the messages from others that click with us, into our lives and then make our own decisions. When we take responsibility for ourselves in this way, we feel like we're living our own life; we're the scriptwriters of our own personal narratives. And we have the power to create lives that are rich tapestries of stories, which our older selves will look back on with fond memories.

Discover your treasure:

1. What resonates with you about this story?
2. Do you feel like the scriptwriter of your own life?
3. Do you set intentions for your life story and how you want it to be?
4. Have you had times when you went along half-heartedly with someone else's decision although it jarred with your values? What happened?
5. Have you had times when you truly knew what was right for you, yet someone else had a different idea? What did you do?
6. Are you prepared to make a stand when something is important to you even if doing so creates conflict?
7. How can you express your truth to other people in a way that doesn't cause them to feel rebuked?
8. How would your life change for the better if you were to decide from here on to truly be the scriptwriter and the director of your own life?

20. SELF-DISCOVERY

L ife was hectic for me as a student and a Mum and, although I had made positive choices about what I wanted to do, I still had the feeling that to some extent I was living somebody else's story. The fourteen year age gap between Ryan's father and me found us negotiating different life stages and cracks were beginning to show once more in the relationship. Tired of arguing, after months of anxiety with sleepless nights, it was clear that the relationship wasn't to be. We separated but agreed to collaborate on raising Ryan. It wasn't easy because I had conflicting values, in which my ideal of raising a child in a stable relationship battled with my principle of being true to myself.

My fractured relationship with Ryan's father was the catalyst for me to begin weekly sessions with the college counsellor, Liz, which provided a welcome outlet for my turbulent emotions. It was the first time that I had ever felt heard and seen for myself, and been given the opportunity to express myself without advice or judgement. Like tidying a cluttered cupboard, Liz helped me to sift through the tangle of thoughts and feelings at the source of the turmoil. She lent me a book called *Games People Play* by Eric Berne about transactional analysis – a psychological theory of personality. It was an eye-opener that enabled me to recognise the subconscious tricks that my own ego had been playing on me. I could also spot places where I had unwittingly participated in the games of others and subconsciously created a few of my own.

One day, on my daily walk home from college through Notting Hill Gate, I stopped at a bookshop, wandered in and made my way to the popular psychology section. It was a mindboggling Aladdin's cave of literature. In anticipation of what would be revealed inside them, I took a selection of books and thumbed through them with nervous excitement. I was immediately grabbed by the lapels and drawn into the texts, unable to stop myself turning the pages. Moments later, I realised that I was sitting on the floor in the bookshop in the popular psychology section with a sense of curiosity and knowingness that I had never before experienced. Where had this wisdom been all of my life? Was it kept for a privileged few? I had never heard my parents, siblings, relatives, friends or teachers talking about anything like this before – and yet it felt like coming home to the truth. I hadn't found myself but I had discovered the maps that would show me the way as I journeyed.

Eventually, I moved out of the apartment in Kensington and went to live in Barnes in South West London. Once my business studies course was finished, I needed to find work. As luck would have it, I was quickly offered the chance to apply for a job in the Head Office of a huge retail fashion company in London. The interview took place on a baking hot July day, when there was a London transport strike that all but brought the city to a halt. The only way for me to get to the office for the interview was to walk – in the hope that there would be a bus or a taxi that I could catch en route. There wasn't.

I walked several miles from Barnes to Oxford Street and arrived thirty minutes late for the interview. Hot and exhausted, I apologised and explained the marathon walk I had just completed. To my surprise, they interviewed me right way. The offices were quiet, but there were several groups of desks where the buying and merchandising teams sat. The groups, I was told, were segregated by garment category – dresses, skirts, blouses and so on – and they had rails of the next season's styles beside them. It seemed like it might be good fun.

Within a few days of the interview the company got in touch to offer me a position. Delighted, I negotiated nevertheless and when we reached an agreement I accepted gratefully. I was glad that I'd made the effort to get through the transport strike and show up.

Life was becoming more stable and my hunger for self-awareness had been ignited. I wanted to be exposed to more consciousness-expanding ideas and concepts – although I wasn't sure what form this would take.

I became increasingly involved with a variety of groups in which people expressed their true feelings and I realised that my latent hunger was for real conversations. The gift of hearing people sharing their stories authentically from their hearts opened *my* heart. It was like coming home to a place inside myself that resonated with the universal truths contained in the refreshing, raw honesty of the group's exchanges.

Once I had finished college, it wasn't feasible for me to continue to see Liz, who had become my trusted counsellor, and so I began to work with an independent therapist called Jan. She created a space for me to speak and be heard. Together, we quickly established that I had a habit of bringing the word 'should' into my decision making. This might have been a legacy of the Catholic sense of duty with which I'd been raised.

'I'm not sure if I *should* do this or that,' I'd say.

Jan would calmly ask, 'I wonder what you'd *like* to do?'

That was a new question for me and invariably catapulted me into an animated response in which I knew exactly what I'd like to do. But was that allowed? Who was this mysterious person that I was waiting for permission from? Learning to eschew the shackles of 'should' and asking myself instead, 'What would I *like* to do?' was liberating.

At the same time I took to journaling. It was the first time I had done any significant writing since school and it was cathartic. Most powerful of all was the clarity and certainty that came to me when my head, heart and gut were aligned. It contrasted with the self-doubt and lack of resolve that came when they were in conflict. Clarity boosted my energy whereas the self-doubt diminished it. Writing enabled me to commit my tussled feelings to the page and then become the witness to my own thoughts when I reread them weeks later. The observer in me became easier to access and my guiding light. It was the beginning of an infinite journey.

That journey began in earnest twenty-five years ago. It has been the catalyst for my training as an NLP Master Practitioner, storyteller and narrative practitioner. I've also amassed close to a thousand personal development books, avidly reading them all at least once and some of them multiple times. How we get onto our own path of self-discovery doesn't matter, but it is important that we do get there – because it offers us the opportunity to shift our perspective and see the world from a more enchanting place. More importantly, we can come to know ourselves and live in a way that is aligned with our personal values and in that way, we can have a truer sense of who we are.

Discover your treasure:

1. What resonates with you about this story?
2. If you're reading this book, the chances are that you're on your own journey of self-discovery – what was the catalyst for that?
3. Who are your inspirers? They might be authors or speakers or workshop leaders or people in your family, work or community or friends and acquaintances.

4. How might it help you to know your own heart, mind and soul better if you wrote about the stories that you're telling yourself on a regular basis?

5. Can you make your witnessing-self – the "you" that observes yourself in a detached way, become your guiding light?

6. Can you notice how some stories that you tell yourself diminish your energy and are therefore disempowering while others brighten your energy and empower you?

7. How could you write more empowering stories about yourself?

21. SYNCHRONICITY

A ustralia is a place I used to dream of visiting, not just in daydreaming moments but when I was sleeping too. Perhaps my desire was sparked by the way that Mary enthused about it after her travels there. Upon her return, she gave me an Australian dollar as a keepsake, which I cherished, promising myself that I would return it one day to Australia, certain that the time would come when I would fly the 10,500 miles to the land of kangaroos and koalas.

It was 1991 and I had just completed my professional marketing exams when I started a new job working in retail fashion advertising. Believing that I'd relish the creative environment, I began my new job with gusto. However, what I should have remembered is that 'retail is detail', as the saying goes, and I'm not a big fan of too much detail. Our working environment consisted of cubicles in an open-plan layout with minimal access to daylight. It was a hot summer in London but, instead of proper air conditioning, we had a noisy machine known as 'the elephant' because of its two grey trunks blowing out slightly cooling air. It wasn't ideal but I decided to stick with the job anyway.

A welcome distraction came in the September when I began dating a new boyfriend. At the time we met, he had already planned to leave the UK the following January on a twenty-month globetrotting expedition, traversing three continents to arrive in Australia by the following June. 'Live for the moment,' I told myself and I refused to think beyond Christmas. However, as January neared, it became impossible to ignore his imminent departure and I had the feeling that it would be a wrench. Twenty months was simply too long to wait for someone to return – we'd both have moved on by then – so we were, I feared, nearing the end of our time together.

We worked in the same vicinity in London and occasionally we'd catch up for lunch. One day, as we chatted in the park over our sandwiches, I heard my voice say, 'How about I meet you in Sydney in June?'

'Great,' was his response and before I knew it I had committed myself to a trip to Australia, the location at the top of my travel wish list. Having no idea how I would pay for the trip – including the flight, accommodation (albeit backpackers' hostels), food and general travel – I decided simply to trust that I'd work it out financially.

Following a fun-filled Christmas, January sped around all too soon and with it a tearful farewell at Heathrow Airport.

Once I'd returned to the heart of London, my first stop was at the travel agents where I booked my flight to Sydney for June, with only a small deposit to pay until March. I was elated to be travelling to the place I had dreamt of.

It's peculiar being in a relationship with somebody who isn't there. In place of the grounded reality in which you spend time together, your connection slips into the realm of fantasy and it effectively becomes a relationship that exists in your mind. On Valentine's Day, when other people were receiving chocolates and roses and planning to celebrate in posh London restaurants, I was just expecting a phone call from somewhere on the African continent. However, I had no sooner arrived home that evening when the doorbell rang and a neighbour handed me a package, saying, 'Claire, I took a delivery for you today.' We chatted briefly before she disappeared and I excitedly tore open the wrapping on the parcel to discover a beautiful red rose with a card that read: 'Out of Africa.' I knew who had arranged it and I was touched.

As my trip to Sydney neared I wasn't sure how I would pay the balance due on the cost of the flight in two weeks' time. Then, one evening, I received a telephone call from Ryan's father. 'The insurance claim has come though,' he said. Two years previously, he, Ryan and I had been involved in a prang on the motorway, and Ryan's father and I had spent that Christmas nursing whiplash injuries and backache. The other driver had been found to be responsible and the insurance company was finally settling our claim. The case had taken such a long time to settle, with no guaranteed outcome, that I had all but forgotten about it.

'Great news,' I said. Then Ryan's father went on to tell me the value of the award that had been allocated to me individually. It was the exact amount of my flight to Sydney. 'That's uncanny – what a coincidence,' I thought, feeling overjoyed by my good luck. It seemed that the Universe had found the exact means for the flight – and with perfect timing. The balance was duly paid and soon I had the precious ticket in my hand.

As the departure day neared I carefully packed a rucksack borrowed from a friend. Thoughts flooded my mind as I prepared: 'How will it be when I land in Sydney? Will it be like it is in my dreams? Will I miss Ryan terribly while he stays in London with his Dad? How are things going to work out with a boyfriend that I haven't seen for six months? And where was that lucky Australian dollar bill…?'

Finally, D-Day arrived and I found myself in a window seat on a vast Boeing 747. Anticipation of the destination and the novelty of being on my first long-haul flight brought butterflies to my stomach. Equipped with audio cassettes, books and the in-flight movie service, the twenty-two hour flight floated by much more quickly than I had imagined it would.

It was evening when the pilot navigated the great 747 onto the runway at Sydney airport and I alighted with the other passengers, elated that I was on Australian soil. Having slept only sporadically during the flight, I was exhausted to the point of being spaced out. Passport stamped and baggage collected, I emerged in the arrivals hall to be greeted by my boyfriend, who had been waiting at the airport since way before the flight was expected. We had a thousand things to talk about as we made our way to the backpackers' hostel in Sydney.

We had planned a trip to Cape Tribulation, Cairns and Port Douglas and he told me he had a surprise in store for me. His father had met up with an old work colleague, who had since emigrated to Australia but who was visiting London. When he had mentioned that his son (my boyfriend) was trekking around Australia, his friend had immediately offered us the opportunity to stay in his house in Port Douglas. It was empty, apart from a house-sitter who stayed there occasionally. 'What great good fortune,' I thought. It seemed like the Universe had gone beyond my wildest dreams with this gift of a wonderful place to stay. We were grateful to have the benefit of the house and appreciated spending several days there, sunning ourselves by the cool blue pool.

The trip to Australia was wonderful – it was all that it had promised to be in my dreams and more as I experienced its raw natural beauty. At the end of June I returned to London, thrilled that I had turned my dream into a story with wonderful memories and grateful for the synchronicity gifted to me by the Universe. And it was a delight to cuddle Ryan again and catch up on what he'd been doing while I was away.

By the time I returned to my job in retail advertising, I was a different person with a renewed sense of accomplishment and broader horizons literally and metaphorically. Ready for something new, I signed up for a Master's Degree in Marketing and after five months I resigned from my job and aged twenty-six I set up my first consultancy, creating business relationships that felt more like partnerships. The future looked bright.

When you want something like I did and you haven't got the means to get it, you have two choices. You can give up on your dreams and rationalise them away, or you can own those dreams and trust the Universe to support you in turning them into real life stories.

Discover your treasure:

1. What resonates with you about this story?
2. Have you got any dreams that you've given up on and if so, how do you feel about those dreams now?
3. Would you be willing to resurrect them and explore whether they feel true for you?
4. Do you feel certain that you want the story that you're dreaming about, with no doubts?
5. Can you own the dream and yet let go of having to *make* the story happen by yourself?
6. Would you be willing to hand the making of your dream story over to the Universe and take whatever steps you can each day, even if you can't yet see how the whole script might unfold?

22. FINDING TRUE LOVE

'Oh my God, what on earth was I thinking?' I thought. Quickly I grabbed a pen and a pad of notepaper and wrote a letter, signed it and folded it carefully, before putting it into an envelope and placing a first-class stamp on it. Slipping out through the front door, I walked rapidly to the red pillar box and pushed the letter through the slot. No turning back now – my message would be delivered the next day. With a huge sigh of relief I turned and walked back home.

Halfway through my Master's Degree, I had taken up a position in the strategic planning department of another huge retailer. The job offered me the security I needed to allow me to focus on my MA and take care of Ryan. It involved the sort of highly analytical, number-crunching work that some people love. I didn't, however, but I could do it – although it wasn't an area in which I was especially gifted or one that I was passionate about. All the same, I was grateful to have work and, as I had the limiting belief that having work that you loved was a pipedream only ever realised by a lucky few, I accepted it gracefully.

The office was air-conditioned and I was seated next to a window, which meant that there was an abundance of natural light, which I appreciated. It had, however, a terribly quiet atmosphere – a contrast indeed to the buzzy buying office where I had begun my retail career and even to the advertising department, which had been relatively lively. Here, I shared an office with three people – two men and a woman who were heads-down people, either by nature or by habit. The office was mostly as quiet as a library, apart from the tapping of keyboards. Speaking wasn't welcomed unless it was about the work.

The place reminded me of a joke that I had heard years earlier about three monks who had taken a vow of silence. Seven years passed and the sound of a cow mooing was heard. One monk broke the silence: 'I think I hear a cow.' Seven years passed and a second responded: 'Yes, me too.' Seven years later the third monk, in frustration, decided it was time to draw the line: 'If you two don't stop talking, I'm leaving!'

I chuckled to myself. Being by this stage in my life more extrovert, I found that this highly analytical, quiet space was a much lower energy place than was ideal for me. Eventually, I bought a pot plant to sit on my desk and its pretty, pink-and-green, variegated leaves lightened up the environment.

Thinking about the letter I'd sent, I was certain it was the right thing to do and, although it might have seemed like a spontaneous action, it was far from that. Most moments of change are the culmination of a journey. After the trip to Australia, the relationship with my then boyfriend had continued as he'd changed his global travel plans. However, two years on, it had turned into a roller-coaster relationship that had eventually become emotionally exhausting for me. I believed that a healthy relationship should be comfortable and life-enhancing for both partners. When relationships became emotionally draining it was time to let them go. Yet I hadn't let go – temporarily, yes, but not decisively – and so the roller-coaster of being in and out of the relationship had ensued, instigated by each of us at different times.

I had eventually become so tired of talking it over and deluding myself that it could work, I had decided that the only way to finally draw a line under it was to write a letter. Now that letter was on its way – and I was at last beginning to reclaim some of the self-esteem that I had invested in trying to make the relationship work, when it would have been obvious to any onlooker that it was way past its sell-by date. I realised that, to be true to yourself, you sometimes have to let go – and that doesn't mean the relationship hasn't had its good times or that either person has to be dubbed 'the bad guy.' Rather, it's that the Universe has even better plans for both people.

Although I had taken ownership of my life several years earlier, I still seemed to be making some decisions that didn't serve my needs. Surely, I thought, it should be as easy to choose what's right for you as to choose what's not right for you? Come to think of it, it must be even easier to choose well rather than unsuitably on our own behalf, because when we go after what we want we are empowered by the motivation to manifest our heart's desire.

When I delved into my psyche, I realised I didn't believe that 'happy ever after' could be a possibility for me – that I could have true love, happiness and abundance or that I deserved those things – especially since I had broken the ultimate Irish Catholic taboo by having my son outside marriage. Granny's messages about the wrath of God must still have been lurking somewhere in my sub-conscious. I also recognised that part of the problem was that I didn't truly know what or who was right for me. It was time to find out and to clear away the blocks to creating the rich tapestry of a joyful life story. I would give myself the space to do it – no relationship entanglements. I was busy enough with work, being a Mum and finishing my MA.

Soon I discovered the power of affirmations and, having studied the work of experts in the field, I began carefully to craft my own. While I could devote a separate book to explaining how I created successful affirmations, here are some golden rules that I stuck to: firstly, the affirmations were in the present tense; secondly, they were true; thirdly, they were inspiring. Now, while those three things might seem contradictory, actually they're not. For example, to attract more money into your life, an affirmation such as

'I'm choosing to live abundantly' would work well because it's present, true and inspiring. Equally, to attract a dream home, an affirmation such as 'I'm now attracting my perfect home into my life' would fulfill the golden rules. My own affirmations evolved as my confidence grew and the statements became more focused. For instance, once I had chosen the apartment I wanted to buy, I created affirmations about that specific place and envisaged myself living there joyfully.

Increasingly aware of the impact of our self-talk on our psyche, I thought back to primary school when we were disciplined by having to write pages of lines as punishment for some misdemeanour. Invariably the sentences we were asked to write affirmed what we children had done wrong. Most popular was: 'I must not be bold.' Thinking about it, why would anyone want to ask children not to be bold? Would we want to encourage them to be shy instead? Fortunately the mind only works in a positive way so when it is told 'I must not be bold,' it focuses on being bold. However, there were other flavours of 'pages of lines' that were downright crazy – when you understand the way the mind works.

For example:

- I must not kick people.
- I must not forget my exercise book.
- I must not swear.
- I must not tell lies.

In these instances, the behaviour didn't change and instead the kicker kicked, the forgetter forgot, the swearer swore and the liar lied. Hopefully, if schools still use this method of reprimanding children, they harness the awesome power of the brain by helping them to affirm good, positive behaviours mindfully.

For instance:

- I choose to treat people with kindness.
- I choose to remember my exercise book.
- I choose to speak to people respectfully.
- I choose to tell the truth.

Getting back to my affirmations – I took them seriously. This meant that after writing them, I recorded them and played them back to myself several times on a daily basis – morning, during the day and last thing at night as I drifted off to sleep.

Around the same time I visited Ireland, having received a heart-warming letter from my father. I had been there occasionally since my son was born, but I had never taken Ryan to the place where I had grown up and now he was eight years old. So it was time to go there with him.

My father had remarried several years earlier and had four stepchildren, two of whom had moved away from home. However, even though only Edel and Tom and two of his stepchildren remained at home, it was crowded. Ryan and I therefore stayed with Uncle Jack and Auntie Eileen (another of my father's sisters), who was visiting from

California on holiday. They both made us feel more than welcome.

As my father had never engaged with Ryan, I was unsure of how he would be with him. One day, Mary and I went with our father and Ryan to tend our Mum's grave. As Mary and I chatted our father marched ahead purposefully, ready to weed and preen. Ryan raced ahead of us, running close behind our father, and began to mimic his walk with his hands behind his back. I noticed and wondered how my father would respond. Would he feel that he was being mocked?

Realising that he had gained a shadow, my father stopped, turned around and waited for Ryan to catch up with him. Then he put his arm around him and they walked like mates to Mum's grave. Now I felt more comfortable that Ryan was becoming integrated into the family that I had grown up in. It became a wonderful farm holiday for Ryan, walking in the fields to count sheep, borrowing my uncle's wellingtons which were much too big for him and riding with his grandfather on the tractor. He was exhilarated.

On our return to England I continued with my affirmations and gradually my life began to change. At work, I was able to move to a different office with new people and a livelier atmosphere. More engaging projects emerged. And, after months of racking my brain to come up with a subject for my MA thesis, an idea presented itself to me. I would explore 'The Perceived Image and Quality of Services', focusing on interior design services. That excited me – it seemed creative and fun.

The only question was how I would get access to good data – the lynchpin of any robust research project. The means presented itself when I realised that one of our sister companies was operating an interior design service as part of its DIY range of home products. The journey to creating a great thesis was only a few internal phone calls away. When I called, the staff at the sister company were more than helpful, giving me permission to interview people, including the management team and the designers involved with the service. To add to the magic, an external consultant who had worked with them on setting up the interior design service became – with the team's blessing – one of my interviewees. There was work to do but it was enjoyable and flowed easily.

As time wore on, I continued with my affirmations habit and the following year I received a pay rise that was beyond my wildest expectations. Although I knew that I deserved to be paid more than I had been earning, I was delighted and grateful. The extra money enabled me to focus on buying an apartment, as I had been renting for several years. Now it looked like I could provide a home of our own for Ryan and myself. Within two months of the pay rise, we moved into a bright, sunny apartment that overlooked a children's playing field in a quiet area. Ryan had two requests only: the bunk beds that I had promised him and that we bring with us his fluffy, black-and-white cat, Charlie, who I had got for him several months earlier. No question – Charlie was coming with us and bunk beds it was.

Shortly afterwards, the opportunity for a job with another company came my way and, upon receiving a wonderful offer that included a car, I jumped ship. Yet my personal life remained quiet. Having committed to remaining single for the time being, I wasn't interested in starting a relationship until I was ready. I had met a few men but I instinctively knew that, although they were great individuals, they weren't right for me, nor was I right for them. I'd stopped looking for the right person and decided to become the right person myself instead. Life had transformed and I was happier than I'd been in a long time.

Then I was in a bookshop one day when I spotted a thin, grey book with the words *30 Days to Find Your Perfect Mate* by Dr Chuck Spezzano on its spine. I took it out and flicked through its thirty chapters, noticing an exercise at the end of each one.

'What would happen if I did all those exercises?' I wondered. I paid for the book and left the shop, intending to do all the exercises as an experiment just for fun. *But* I nevertheless committed to doing them fully.

There was a contact telephone number for something called Psychology of Vision at the back of the book, for information on talks and workshops by Dr Chuck Spezzano. I called, joined the mailing list and in less than a week a flyer came in the mail: 'Sex, Drugs & Rock 'n' Roll – What's Next?' It advertised an evening talk by Chuck Spezzano and Lency Spezzano at Regent's College in London.

'I'm going,' I decided.

Upon arriving at the college, I made my way upstairs to the talk. As I stood around in the crowded reception room I wasn't sure what to do and soon it was time for everyone to pile into the lecture room. There was a sea of people, so I stood at the back, suitably close to the door. Chuck and Lency were so far away at the front of the room that I couldn't see them clearly.

Chuck began to speak about the best thing since sex, drugs and rock 'n' roll – a model for living called Psychology of Vision. What he said was a revelation to me; it offered a new perspective on life and relationships, one that was loving, empowering and healing. Then Lency spoke and she was the sweetest person I'd ever seen or heard – so gentle and yet so profound.

I came away from that talk knowing that 'happy ever after' wasn't just for fairy tales – it was a mindset. I had already experienced a seismic shift in my thinking and energy over the ten months since sending the letter to my ex-boyfriend. So now I resolved to create space in my world for the perfect relationship.

Meanwhile, I did the exercises in the book religiously, letting go energetically of old boyfriends and relinquishing gifts I'd received from them to the charity shop. I let go of all my teenage crushes and even those below the radar ones on celebrity movie stars. I continued too with the affirmations.

And...what happened? Did it work? Did I find my perfect mate in thirty days?

Well, the answer is simple: no! It took about six weeks – more like forty-two days.

I already knew David – we had danced together at a Christmas party to the 1994 popular chart-hit version of 'Love is All Around' by the group Wet Wet Wet. When we met again at a barbeque I was already immersed in the thirty-days-to-find-your-perfect-mate programme. That evening we reconnected and it seemed inevitable that we would be together. David was going on holiday the next day but promised to call me upon his return.

He did call me when he got back and we started dating. The first time we went out to dinner together, our conversation was delightfully easy as we chatted animatedly over the table. Then David asked me a question: 'What do you look for in a man?'

'Good question,' I replied. 'Someone who tells me what he's feeling.'

'Well, right now,' he said, in a matter of fact way, 'I'm feeling quite intimidated by you.'

I was ashamed to think that I might be behaving in a way that triggered those feelings in him. Beyond that, though, I was amazed by the courage he showed in sharing his vulnerability with me – and doing this in a way that was not 'needy', just raw and honest. In that moment of real conversation he won my heart.

It was a whirlwind romance and after three weeks we moved in together, although he was initially reluctant to abandon the house he had just bought to spend most of his time at my apartment. We enjoyed being in each other's company and would find ourselves chatting and laughing for hours.

After five weeks David asked me to marry him. I knew that the answer was yes and ten months later we got married on the beautiful Island of Mauritius, in a boutique hotel on the beach in a place called Trou d'Eau Douce.

Learning to love myself and discover what was right for me had transformed my energy and my self-esteem, and led to my having a greater ability to recognise what I wanted and what was right for me. I was propelled into resonating at a new vibration in the world and my inner barometer became more sensitive to my needs. Being more connected to my inner wisdom also enabled me to become more emotionally available for a relationship and therefore I attracted someone who was available for me.

Finding true love begins with self-love and honouring our heart's desires. That's not about self-indulgence at the expense of other people but it is about acknowledging that some things are true for us yet others are not. Life is easier and more fulfilling when we identify what resonates with us – that's the clue and then we can let go of what is not for us while recognising that it might be exactly right for someone else.

As **Polonius** says in Shakespeare's *Hamlet*:

This above all – to thine own self be true,

And it must follow, as the night the day,

Thou canst not then be false to any man.

Discover your treasure:

1. What resonates with you about this story?
2. How easily do you let go of what's not working in your life?
3. Have you found yourself thinking that if only you worked harder at a relationship or work or a business, it would come right?
4. How well connected are you to your inner barometer that tells you when to continue and when to quit?
5. Can you let people, places and things go with love and gratitude in order to create space for what's new?
6. How much time do you spend identifying the stories you are telling yourself by noticing your own inner dialogue?
7. Do you recognize that these stories that you are telling yourself are shaping your life for worse or for better?
8. How would it enhance your life if you were to transform your disempowering stories into more empowering ones by changing what you believe about yourself, others and the world?

23. AUTHENTIC WAY

I t was June 2001 and I was flying with American Airlines from London to Los Angeles to attend a Medical Congress in Anaheim in California. I had been working in marketing with a multinational pharmaceutical giant since 1998 and we were about to launch a new drug in September 2001. Initially I loved the job – it felt like we were helping to change lives for the better and it had the creativity and balance of communication that I enjoyed. It was right for me.

However, three years on, the workload was never ending and human resources were thin on the ground. The company had merged with another corporation the previous year and the newly conjoined enterprise was only just beginning to settle down. Although I was based in England, it was an American company and like many others they had adopted the 'more for less' mantra. Following the merger, the usual turf wars, politics and cliques surfaced as people strategically chose how to play their cards in order to achieve optimal personal outcomes for themselves.

I was working sixty-hour weeks as standard, which meant that David and I were like ships in the night as, working in information technology, he also had an intense schedule. Cooking dinner became my break from work for two hours before resuming it again in a self-created evening shift that regularly finished at midnight or at one o'clock in the morning.

Our social life had gone by the wayside and it was a struggle to find the time to take a holiday. We occasionally grabbed weekend breaks – never a proper chance to relax and unwind. By now, David, Ryan and I were living in Northamptonshire, in a house situated at the edge of an old market town that sat on the brow of a hill, overlooking a patchwork of green fields for miles. However, we rarely had a moment to absorb the beauty of the countryside.

Instead, here I was – on yet another business trip. In truth, I enjoyed the flight to LA: we were allowed to travel business class for transatlantic flights and nobody could call or email me while I was flying high. I finished off some more work and then, as time wore on, I kicked back to watch a movie. It was *The Legend of Bagger Vance*, based on the book by Steven Pressfield and adapted as a screenplay by Jeremy Levin. As an added bonus, the movie starred Matt Damon and Will Smith. I was happy.

In *The Legend of Bagger Vance*, Matt Damon plays a golfer Rannulph Junah who has lost his edge since returning from

World War I. He has become withdrawn from life and estranged from his sweetheart. He finds himself invited to take part in a golf tournament and Will Smith, in the guise of Bagger Vance, becomes his caddy. The turning point comes when Bagger Vance helps him to recognise that what's missing is his 'Authentic Swing'.

Watching the movie intently to see what happened next, I noticed the air steward hovering over me to collect the movie player. Was she nuts? - There were ten minutes to go before the end. Time to negotiate. 'Can I please watch the last ten minutes of this movie?' I asked. Reluctantly, she agreed. Phew!

I watched as Matt Damon's character – Junah - took part in a big tournament but still hadn't found his elusive swing. The game continued and it looked like he might get beaten. But then…it happened: he rediscovered his own unique swing and – *voilà!* – he won both the tournament and his sweetheart.

I switched off the movie player and handed it back to the air steward as I thought about the idea of an authenticity that we bring to the world – our own way that is the truth for us? Could I have an authentic way and, if so, what might it be? It seemed idealistic but I was hopeful for the first time in a long while that I could find a better way to live.

In the corporate world people are taught to be generalists because then they are versatile. These human resources can then be deployed more readily to pick up the slack. However, while deploying human beings as human resources might be good for productivity and profitability, it is not good for the soul. It was not good for me and I knew that something needed to change.

After some further soul searching, I recognised that I had modified myself to fit into a corporate role. I had become an 'I'll be your anything you want me to be' person and I was addicted to performing and getting exceptional appraisals from my bosses. I was running on a belief system that taking on the world was laudable and that I was a hero for doing it. I loved telling people that I was working twelve-hour days as standard and that my workload was bigger than most people's. I looked with contempt on people who didn't have a similar 'work ethic' to mine.

Watching that movie definitely sowed some seeds, yet I still went back to the same crazy environment that acted as a breeding ground for my overworking behaviour. A few months earlier while flying to the US, I had watched a video of an American coach who was regarded by many as a 'Business Guru' and who advised that, in order to be successful, you needed to be focused on your goals to the exclusion of everything else – which meant not spending meaningless time at family events or with friends. I remember thinking, 'Oh, good to hear that – sounds like I'm on track!'

So I continued working mad hours and, after 9/11 in September 2001, we launched the product. Added stress came from travelling by air at a time when everyone was understandably nervous. In October 2001, I found myself in Italy with responsibility for a group of physicians from the UK who were attending a medical congress in Verona. The war in Afghanistan broke out while we were there and on the day we were due to return 'no authorisation to fly' messages were issued by the company I worked for. There I was, with a group of medical professionals who desperately wanted to return to their clinics, while I frantically tried to get company clearance to board the flight. To my relief, we did get back to the UK that day and then it was back to business as usual.

The crazy pace of work continued. However, it started to take its toll on me and that January I was forced to take time out from work with flu. I returned too early, only to find myself relapsing. After a bit more recovery time, I was soon back up to full speed again. However, I wasn't happy. I was running fast to keep up in the rat race and not really living.

In addition, since the merger the company had switched from individual offices to an open-plan layout – mainly to maximise the use of space. The space allocated per person was tiny and every day felt like a game of space invaders. You daren't push your chair back too vigorously or you could go careering into the person behind you. The physical proximity of people, coupled with the barrage of conversations going on around me, was perplexing. It was the complete antithesis of the quiet office that I had shared several years before at the retail company and way too much stimulation for me. It was a daily drain on my energy.

In the middle of that year a take over of the company by another, even larger pharmaceutical giant was announced, throwing everyone into further disarray and upping the ante even more on competitiveness and self interest. I knew that this environment was not good for me and David was feeling the same way about his work. That, combined with the fact that the new company offices would have required us to move to another part of the UK, led to our deciding to set up a business together in which we could combine our skills and, more importantly, create a working environment that we believed in. By the end of September I had resigned from the company. I was sad that work I had once loved had become crazy and overwhelming, and I felt inadequate that I couldn't keep on taking on more while handling it easily.

Yet the sense of liberation after leaving the company was wonderful. Initially, the exhaustion I had been suppressing surfaced and for three weeks I couldn't get enough sleep. David and I set up our first business with a group of others, but a few months down the line we all agreed to go our separate ways.

Although I was completely comfortable with the decision we'd made, I did wonder what I was going to do next to earn money. When I arrived home one day, the answer-phone light was flashing and I listened to the message: 'Hello, this is a message for Claire Taylor. I have an opportunity that you might be interested in. Please call me back.' There was a telephone number.

'What's somebody trying to sell me now?' I wondered. I called the number all the same, only to discover that the caller was a head hunter who was enquiring if I'd be interested in a consultancy opportunity. I was – and the very next day I went to meet the company; the day after that we negotiated the contract and I began the project the following Monday.

That was the beginning of my career as a marketing consultant in healthcare, and I was grateful to have control over my own work, time and environment at last. Soon I began to have a life as well as a career.

Although there was a dramatic improvement in my work–life balance, I still didn't feel as though I'd found my authentic self. I questioned whether the work I was doing was aligned with my values. I was constantly racked by the negative publicity that the pharmaceutical industry was getting and I'd ask myself: 'Is there a better way to manage people's health rather than using medicines?'

I was still immersed in the world of personal development, continuing to amass tons of literature that I read with interest. However, I also began to study alternative medicine practices and trained as a Neurolinguistic Programming Master Practitioner. Then I took on three years of study in nutritional therapy. The nature of the consultancy work gave me the flexibility to study, take exams and do the clinical hours required for the course.

In spite of my own questioning of the industry that I'd been involved in, I was always amazed when some fellow nutrition students would say to me, 'oh, are you moving to the other side now?' It was as if some saw healthcare purely in terms of a political battleground between big bad pharma versus the wholesome innocence that they attributed to complementary practices. I was intrigued by the conspiracy stories that people who were entrenched in either natural healthcare practices or medicines created about each other. However, these entrenched positions seemed to me to be more concerned with taking the moral high ground and being 'right' – and not about healing. These attitudes were, I feared, coming from the ego and not from the heart.

'Surely there's only one side – helping people to get well and stay well?' I'd reply.

Yet I juggled with these two healthcare modalities for several years before coming to the conclusion that healthcare is as complicated as human beings are. There is no one right answer for everybody. Integration seems to be the most enlightened way forward – and integration means different things to different people. For some people, it means taking a more natural approach, while for others it's a more medical way. So it's not just about integrated medicine; it's about person-centred integrated medicine.

I eventually healed my own split mind about healthcare modalities and, despite thinking that it was time to move on from my healthcare marketing work into something that seemed more spiritual, I had a continuous flow of consultancy work. 'That's a message,' I thought and eventually I understood the message:

All work is spiritual work and enlightenment is about how we bring ourselves to our work. I realised that, in the ten years since I had left the pharmaceutical company in

2002, I had changed. I was more open hearted, lighter, more willing to be vulnerable and more authentic than my younger self had been. I was more able to show love (as my Mum would say) without getting caught up in the needs of my ego. Showing love is not about being sweet all the time – that's just personality – showing love is about whether you're operating from your ego or your heart. Are you scoring points to make yourself look smart or are you working collaboratively for the best outcome for the project and all concerned? It is not about being everyone's best friend – it is about being effective while having respect and compassion for other people.

I found myself setting intentions of a different kind – based on collaboration, partnership, communication, creative solutions and joy. When I felt the energies of competition, attack or defensiveness welling up in myself or other people, I saw it as an opportunity to heal something in myself, in a group and even in the world.

I was now doing work that wasn't a million miles away from what I had been doing ten years earlier. If anything, it had the potential to be even more stressful as it involved leading teams, working internationally and multiculturally and at even more senior levels with organisations. However, as I realised that the route to success lay in transforming myself and bringing my authentic self to my work, the work itself had more joy, ease and flow.

Our giftedness may be something that we do brilliantly, such as singing or writing or mathematics or sports, and it's good to know what those gifts are so that we can leverage them. I believe that our authentic way is about how we bring ourselves to anything. When we're closed, defensive, competitive, playing roles, insisting on being right and making everyone else wrong, we're not being authentic – that's not who we are. When we're being open, vulnerable, playful, curious and speaking our truth while respecting and valuing others, we're bringing the true essence of ourselves, unmasked, to the people we interact with day to day.

It is not about using positive thinking to pretend that all is well in an attempt to mask our pain, nor is it about being a pessimistic nay-sayer who stubbornly refuses to integrate anything into our lives that wasn't invented in our own psyche. Bringing our authentic self to our work and our lives is about unmasking who we really are and bringing our unique energy to the world – recognising what resonates and trusting what is true for us.

There is a **Zen** saying:

> Before enlightenment, chop wood, carry water. After enlightenment chop wood, carry water.

Discover your treasure:

1. What resonates with you about this story?
2. Do you feel that you can bring the authentic 'you' to your work or does it feel safer to live by a script created by other people?
3. Do you know who you really are or have you danced to someone else's tune for so long that you've forgotten?

4. Are you able to step back from your work and think about how it's working for you?

5. Do you feel nourished by your work or are you constantly in fight-or-flight mode, battling against deadlines and politics?

6. Can you make healthy boundaries and limits so that your work feels like a win–win partnership between you and those you work with or serve?

7. What changes would you be prepared to commit to which would create the space for you to discover your authentic self?

24. A WAY WITH WORDS

On a recent business visit to Zurich I was meditating in my hotel room at the end of the day when I decided to invite more wonderful positive synchronicity and guidance into my life. The familiar phrase 'be careful what you ask for' crossed my mind.

Returning home the next day, I went to the check-in desk, juggling my bags and waving my boarding card about in my hand as I rummaged in my handbag for my passport. The attendant at the desk – a jolly, relaxed, middle-aged chap – spoke with a Swiss–German accent but in a warm and friendly way, untypical of the Swiss formality that I had come to expect.

'Just let me have the boarding pass,' he smiled.

I gave it to him and continued the search until eventually my passport emerged, which I presented to him.

'No, I don't need that,' he said. 'Just what you had in your hand already is all I need. You see,' he continued, 'life is like that – sometimes you already have everything you need right there in your hand but you don't know it.'

'Wow,' I thought, 'that's profound.'

Then he said, '*Conasatatu.*'

I was puzzled, wondering why he was speaking in another language to me. My confusion must have shown on my face, for then he said, 'Ah! But you are Irish, I thought you would understand this?' Immediately, I realised that he had actually said, '*Conas tá tú?*' which means 'how are you?' in Gaelic.

I smiled in turn and responded, '*Go maith!*' which means 'good'. 'How do you know the Gaelic language?' I asked.

'My forefathers were Irish,' he said. Then, looking at me in earnest, he continued, 'This language and culture is disappearing fast. It's people like you and me who must keep it alive.'

I nodded and said, 'Yes,' which I followed with, '*Go n-éirí an bóthar leat.*' Noticing his quizzical look, I immediately added, 'It's an Irish way of saying goodbye and literally means "may the road rise with you".'

Rubbing his arms, he replied, 'Oh my goodness, that's just given me goose bumps! Please say it again.'

'*Go n-éirí an bóthar leat,*' I repeated as I picked up my cabin baggage to go.

'*Sláinte,*' he said. This means 'health' and is another way to say goodbye in Gaelic, although it's also used when people clink glasses in a toast like 'cheers'.

'*Slán agus beannacht,*' I replied: goodbye and bless you.

I headed towards the gate to catch my flight, pondering the rich metaphorical language of Ireland – the country where I had grown up, the land of my ancestors. As I boarded the flight, I cast my mind back to a conversation I'd had several years earlier, when I had been a corporate employee. I remembered sitting opposite my former boss in a glass-walled office and shifting uncomfortably in my seat as he said: 'This company values succinctness.' I felt berated for using too many words when I was speaking. My heart sank. 'Why?' I thought, feeling irritated and ashamed that I somehow might be considered inadequate. 'Is there a global shortage of words? Are we about to run out of them? Has the finance department done a cost-per-spoken-word analysis and issued a daily quota per person?'

As a lover of language and words, to be told that I must use them sparingly threw me into a disconcerting dilemma. Naturally, I wanted people to think of me as a good and professional communicator, but to reduce my speech to bullet points seemed an assassination of communication.

As I sat buckled into my seat on the flight from Zurich to London, I pondered the notion that I had rarely seen people express their personal feelings within corporate organisations, as most employees quickly learn that being diplomatic, factual and wholeheartedly positive is the most appropriate way to be. It seemed to me that there was little room for emotional honesty in business conversations – this was reserved for conversations in the kitchen or around the water cooler. I had seen people resign from companies rather than appear vulnerable or be branded a whinger if they raised an issue about what wasn't working. It was a blight on office life that meant the truth remained unspoken for many. When I resigned from an organisation after reaching my own breaking point, I had also been afraid of being regarded as vulnerable and weak. I had felt that there was no space in the corporation for the story of what I was experiencing because it wasn't joyful – and so I had kept it to myself. I didn't want to admit to the messiness of feelings. As in my own case, I now suspected that a chronic masking of emotion and untold stories contributed to the stress that many people experienced in organisations.

It still seems to me that many organisations don't really listen to what their employees are saying because that takes time. Moreover, listening without judgement is not what people in the business world are generally trained to do. We're expected to have good judgement and pride ourselves on it. We can cut to the chase and get decisions made rapidly. It's all about being constantly active and even hyped. Succinctness is often valued over stories that take us on a deeper journey beyond the cognitive level. Succinct saves time – but at the cost of truly honest conversations. For that reason, I'm an advocate for the power of story in business and in life.

Ireland is a country where people have always told stories and there is a musicality to its lilting language. It is the home of an astonishing host of extraordinary writers, poets and musicians. As Ireland is the land of my birth, it's perhaps no surprise that the magic of language courses through my veins and in every cell of my body. So, while my head was hearing the message about 'succinctness' in that meeting with my ex-boss, my heart certainly wasn't buying into the concept of being so economical with words.

Words are intriguing, extraordinary and incredibly powerful! I have always loved them and used them abundantly as a guilt-free indulgence. Connecting words together to create wonderful sentences jam-packed with meaning is sheer joy to me!

As a child at school, I was awed by the art of alliteration and delighted when I discovered onomatopoeia, after which I began to notice 'sizzling sausages' and the 'rat-tat' of rain pattering on the windows. The first poem, beyond nursery rhymes, that I ever learned was about the kindness of Trees. It was strange to tie trees and kindness together in the same sentence and yet perfect because trees do seem to be pretty benevolent, in the absence of strong gales.

As juniors at school, we were asked to write 'compositions' in our special books. These were stories or essays with space at the beginning to draw a picture. I loved writing compositions and then reflecting the story with crayoned images. Even when I moved on to 'big' school, I was excited when the teacher asked us to write essays and thought it odd when friends didn't enjoy it in the same way that I did. I have to confess that I was significantly less enthused when the teacher asked us to complete a page of mathematics homework.

Like many children, I loved stories and especially to have them read to me, as I was engaged by the essence captured in few simple sentences. When I was a child of seven, fairy tales were a great favourite of mine, especially those written by Sinéad de Valera, who was wife of Éamon de Valera – the third president of Ireland. She wasn't a public figure and I had no idea what her political views were and cared even less. She was a primary school teacher who wrote children's stories that I relished. Each story was laced with fairy folk and held a moral for the reader.

When I was nine years old, the most memorable book I read was *Snowflake* by Paul Gallico – a story about the life of a snowflake that was an allegory of human life. Although I was only a child, that book had an extraordinary impact on me, moving me to tears for which I had no conscious explanation. Paul Gallico's use of language was so powerful that I was captivated on an unconscious level by both beauty and sadness.

Later, as I have already mentioned, I was whisked off down the corridors of Malory Towers and St Clare's in Enid Blyton's boarding school adventures of teenage minxes who played tricks on unsuspecting adults. Then, as a fifteen-year old, I was taken with a character called Touchstone in Shakespeare's comedy *As You Like It*. Touchstone was the fool or the clown who liked to quibble with words. Some of the best Touchstone quibbles are:

The fool doth think he is wise but the wise man knows himself to be a fool.

and –

Let us make an honourable retreat.

Touchstone was like a Shakespearian Monty Python character and he even coined the everyday phrase 'with bag and baggage' – whatever that means? Perhaps it refers to both the physical and emotional burdens we carry with us.

When I was an older teenager, proverbs became the tools with which my brother William and I created a little Touchstone magic of our own. We'd fuse proverbs together and then laugh – real belly laughs – at our new combinations. These were moments where you really had to be there to find it funny. Instead of 'a rolling stone gathers no moss' and a 'faint heart never won a fair lady', we liked 'a rolling stone never won a fair lady'. Instead of 'every dog has his day' and 'everything comes to him who waits', our version was 'every dog comes to him who waits'. I don't know what actually happens in those moments of silliness, where two or more people are locked in belly-aching laughter, but it is a truly magical connection that to onlookers must seem like glorious insanity.

It was in adulthood that I began to learn more about the vibrational power of words. Initially, this was a completely personal and unexamined experience. Listening to language that was aggressive, vulgar or just plain negative made me feel bad, while hearing positive uplifting words and phrases and ideas raised my spirits. It's not rocket science, everyone knows that words are powerful, even children.

Japanese author Dr Masaru Emoto has written a wonderful book called *The Hidden Messages in Water*, in which he explains the results of experiments he conducted to show how the vibrations of words influence the way that water crystallises. Positive loving words uttered over glasses of water which were then frozen created stunning crystals, while negative words begot misshapen ones.

Over the years I have worked with many of the world's leading advertising agencies and I've often been asked, 'What kind of advertising communications really appeal to you?'

My response is always the same: 'I can be captivated by a great line of copy – they don't come along often, but when I see one I know it because it connects with me in a way that is beyond words.'

Two years after that conversation about succinctness, I trained in NLP (Neurolinguistic Programming) and I remember the sheer delight and excitement I felt as the trainer took us through the magic of metaphor and linguistics. It confirmed what I knew in my heart about the power of a good story.

The flight from Zurich was now coming in to land at Heathrow and it was time for me to reclaim my baggage and return home. David had come to meet me at the airport, which was a delight. When I got home, there waiting for me was a copy of the book *The Hero's Journey* by Stephen Gilligan and Robert Dilts. I had recently completed a 'Hero's Journey' four-day weekend workshop run by the authors in the Cotswolds and I had ordered the book afterwards.

Interestingly, they speak a great deal about how language and metaphor speak not just to our conscious mind but reach beyond it to resonate with our subconscious selves.

The desk attendant in Zurich talked about how he had goose bumps when he heard the phrase '*go n-éirí an bóthar leat*'. Somewhere in his psyche, it was as if he held an ancestral memory of that wonderful metaphorical language. Of course, the phrase doesn't just mean goodbye – it has an extraordinary energetic and visual power. Saying it, is to wish somebody ease and success on their journey not only on the way home but in their life as well.

Thinking about the power of metaphor, I recalled a beautiful Gaelic poem by Séamus Ó Néill that I learnt at school when I was twelve years old. It touched me in such a special way that it has always stayed with me. I shared it a few years ago with my brother-in-law Mike when his and Mary's girls were small. He was passionate about teaching them Gaelic and would often speak the language to them.

Subh Milis

Bhí subh milis
Ar bhaschrann an dorais
Ach mhúch mé an corraí
Ionam d'éirigh,
Mar smaoinigh mé ar an lá
A bheas an baschrann glan,
Agus an láimh bheag
Ar iarraidh.

This translates to:

There was jam
On the door handle
But I suppressed the anger
That rose up in me,
Because I thought of the day
That the door handle would be clean
And the little hand
Would be gone.

The poet is telling a story about finding sticky jam on the door handle when he went to grasp it. Ugh! And then, before getting annoyed about it, he stopped and realised that the mess on the door handle came with the gift of small children and that clean door handles would mean that the children had grown up and flown the nest.

Perhaps it's also a metaphor for when our lives seem messy. It's good to know that this is often because we have woven rich tapestries of experience in our lives, rather than living with the sterility of the perfect order that was extolled as the essence of godliness when I was at boarding school.

So, let's return once more to the corporate message that had thrown me into a dilemma: 'This company values succinctness.' I had explored and now reached my own conclusions about the places for succinctness and for story.

Firstly, on succinctness – it has a place for sure: as Einstein said, 'If you can't explain it simply, you don't understand it well enough;' so making up a story to whitewash over a lack of knowledge is a misuse of the art. If you want to communicate effectively then sending a longwinded epistle by email is not a good choice. It's best to keep these sorts of communication brief and, to that end, even pick up the phone and have a conversation when you can – too much time is wasted in the ping-pong of often incomprehensible emails.

'Death by 100 busy slides' is another corporate phenomenon that most of us in the business world have experienced. It often occurs in presentations when dozens of slides burdened with mind-boggling narrative are flashed before our eyes. Here, being succinct works visually. However, when you want to inspire people nothing is more powerful than engaging them verbally with a story. These are places where succinctness and story make for good bedfellows.

When we speak to people, succinctness is a tool to communicate facts but it is not a tool for real conversations. It tells you nothing of the inner dialogue that a person is holding with him – or herself, which reflects what they are really thinking and feeling, and what they truly believe and value. Until you know what is going at these levels for the individuals within an organisation, you're not fully communicating with them and real change remains impossible.

In our conversations, we also need to overcome the limiting staccato of bullet points that our cognitive, driven and time-pressured world has created – as if humans were industrial robots. As I have mentioned previously, the space for real conversation in our work environments is limited reducing the scope for open and honest communication. A factor in this may be a corporate fear of the emotional indulgence that might ensue if people are given a chance to speak freely. However, self-expression is not about emotional indulgence. It's about listening carefully to the story, which both reveals the surface message and throws light on the deeper underlying belief systems. Stories are the means through which we gain access to that rich information, since they are a window to our beliefs, values and self-concepts.

Communication is not just about the words; it's about the energy that is exchanged between individuals. Just like tennis doesn't just happen on its own between the players' rackets, conversation is an exchange between two minds, bodies and energy systems. Great communication requires time, space and intelligent use of language that is spoken, physical and energetic. That nameless 'something' that happens when two people communicate is the Tao of storytelling – it's the essence of a genuine connection.

So let's celebrate the richness of story, metaphor and poetry that allows us to communicate with each other at a deep level of connection and energy; while using succinctness to bring simplicity and clarity where needed.

Discover your treasure:

1. What resonates with you about this story?
2. Think about your communication – how easy do you find it to express yourself honestly in particular environments?
3. Consider some of the best conversations that you've had: what was the nature of them, where did they take place, who was involved and what made the conversation memorable?
4. How can you combine the use of story, metaphor and succinctness in your communications to benefit both you and the other person or people?
5. How can you create the space to listen to the richness of another's story – and aim to do so more frequently.
6. How has listening enhanced your understanding of other peoples' perspectives?
7. What can you do differently on a regular basis that will continue to enhance your communications with other people?

25. HIDDEN GIFTS

'You're so lazy, you could spend all day doing nothing,' my Mum told me often. It's true that I could spend hours wandering around in my pyjamas, appearing to do nothing. However, I was never doing 'nothing'. I was daydreaming.

One day, when I was eleven years old, Mum came home from shopping in Galway and said, 'I've a gift for you.' I was excited and touched, as she didn't often do surprises. Then, from her bag, she took a six-by-four-inch wooden plaque with a tiny hole in the top through which to hang it on the wall. She handed it to me. I turned it the right way up and saw it had some words on it and a cartoon painted in black:

How beautiful it is to do nothing

And then rest afterwards.

There was a cartoon of man lying on a chaise longue. I felt ashamed and I laughed nervously.

'Let's have a look, let's have a look!' William and Mary crowded around. 'Ha, ha, ha!' they laughed, 'that's perfect for you.'

My father thought it was riveting. In fact, so much so, that even now – donkey's years later – he often reminds me of it since it features amongst his top ten favourite stories, which he always tells anew as if he'd never told them before. He begins, 'Do you ever remember, Claireen, about that plaque that we got you that said: "How beautiful it is to do nothing and then rest afterwards"?'

'Yes, Dad, I remember,' I say.

'I always thought it was so funny,' he says, and goes on to remind me about how lazy they thought I was.

'Thanks, Dad!'

Secretly, I quite liked the plaque and it hung on my bedroom wall for many years. Yet at the same time it was a constant reminder that I believed my Mum thought I was a lazy sloth. She bought me extra school books so that I could be ahead of the curve, especially maths books since I found maths so utterly boring. She told me: 'If you finish your maths book, I will buy you a special present and you can choose what you like.' Gosh, I was motivated to begin with but, night after night spent doing those extra maths sessions soon became a drag, and so I never finished the maths book and never got that special present.

It drove me nuts that she always wanted me to do housework – to wash the dishes, clean the bathroom or polish the furniture. Whenever I did, she would say that

I hadn't done the task properly, which was probably true because I was a child and not interested in cleaning and polishing. Sometimes she would attempt to motivate me with a promise of pocket money in return for jobs. When I had finished she would review the jobs and, needless to say, I had never completed them to the standard she expected and so I never got my full reward. In fact, the reason that I could never do these sorts of tasks well enough was that I was bored by them before I'd even begun. Mary in comparison, did everything almost perfectly and so did much better in the rewards stakes.

At the same time I had a passion. I loved creative writing and would come home from school delighted if we had been given an English essay or a poem to write for homework. From the moment the homework was announced, I would greet it with excitement and carry that feeling all the way home, bursting to begin. Occasionally, I would even do some of my sister's creative homework projects on my own behalf (she did them herself too), as well as the essays, poems and drawings that I had been set. I handed them all in at school, as we had the same teacher. The teacher didn't mind marking the occasional extra poem, essay or drawing that resulted when my creativity had become overzealous.

However, as I grew older I became more conscious and ashamed of being an incorrigible daydreamer. I saw it as a huge character defect, something that needed to be eradicated. I never, ever allowed any of my corporate colleagues to see me daydreaming, although I secretly noticed that my best ideas and work came after a powerful daydreaming session and that they always loved the results. Still, I thought it was all about focus and being alert. 'The world needs more "lerts",' I would often joke.

You don't need to be a psychologist to decipher the message and pattern that I had encoded in my subconscious: *'Daydreaming is a useless activity done by lazy people. Lazy daydreamers don't do things properly and therefore don't deserve any rewards.'*

At the turn of the millennium, I knew that I needed to get away from the kind of corporate work that had taken over my life. Through working so hard, I was trying to compensate for what I believed to be true about me: that I was a lazy daydreamer who constantly needed to kick my own ass in order to keep me 'doing' 'doing' 'doing'. Appraisals of my work were top-notch because I'd mastered the art of doing everything so perfectly that I'd get the reward. The idea of achieving anything less than an 'Exceeds Expectations' grade in my appraisals became unthinkable to me. I was once delighted to earn a grade of 'Exceptional' and to learn that, as a result, my bonus percentage would be amongst the highest in the entire UK affiliate of the company that year.

It took me a long time to realise that I was still trying to please my Mum by finding and then excelling in highly challenging corporate environments within large multinationals. To be considered exceptional in that environment was, to my indefatigable inner people-pleaser, a real vote of confidence.

However, I was in a huge quandary because, whenever I thought about doing the creative things that made my heart sing (and as I rose the corporate ladder those opportunities became more rare), an inner voice would rear its ugly head and say, 'That's not work, there's no money in it. You can't make a living out of those airy-fairy ideas, it's irresponsible.' I worked with several great coaches on releasing myself from the grips of my dilemma, but my progress was slow because I wasn't aware then of the subconscious structure that was creating that internal tug of war for me. I could never admit that, beneath the competent exterior that I had learned to convey, I believed there lurked a lazy daydreamer waiting to escape.

It took another ten years for me to allow myself to create any significant space in my life for creativity – and especially for writing. One evening, shortly after I had started to write my original story blog, I sat down with David to watch the movie *P.S. I Love You*, based on the book written by Irish author Cecelia Ahern. Although aware of the book and the movie, I had never engaged with either until that evening. It's a sweet story and beautifully captured in the movie – a real tear-jerking chick-flick. And so I sat on the sofa with David and blubbed my way through it.

As I knew that Cecelia Ahern had written *P.S. I Love You* when she was in her early twenties and still a student, I was curious to read up on what she'd been doing since. So I googled her name and found a YouTube video interview with her. In it, she described her early days as a writer and recounted her experience of 'sitting at the kitchen table at home in my pyjamas, writing *P.S. I Love You* when I was still at college'. She went on to describe herself as a daydreamer in a completely nonchalant, 'that's just me' kind of way. I gasped to myself. I could hear my internal critic saying, 'You sat at the kitchen table in your pyjamas, writing? You're actually admitting that you are a daydreamer, like it's something to be proud of?'

My puzzled mind at this stage jumped to: 'But... you're an extraordinarily successful writer.'

And then to: 'Wow, maybe I could trust my inner daydreamer and enjoy it with curiosity? Perhaps I don't need to start a twelve-step group – like alcoholics anonymous – to help daydreamers like me to get over ourselves.'

Instead, I could accept and welcome the gift that had always been there. 'Maybe it's okay sometimes to sit around in pyjamas, daydreaming and writing,' I thought.

After all, it made so much sense, because when the creative muse strikes there isn't always time to get dressed. My muse doesn't care what I'm wearing: when I'm in a creative flow I know that the only thing the muse cares about is whether I can get whatever is coming through on to the page as quickly as is humanly possible, even if inspiration turns up in the middle of the night.

And so, listening to Cecelia Ahern's story of writing the first of her many novels, I was inspired and I realised that there is actually a great wisdom in that plaque given to me by my Mum and that, perhaps, is subconsciously why my Dad, bless him, reminds me of it every time I go to Ireland:

How beautiful it is to do nothing

And then rest afterwards.

The wisdom is that it is only when we can stop obsessively 'doing' mundane things in an insane dance of constant motion that we can create the space to be, to connect with our creativity and with the answers that we seek. Once we have tapped into the juice of creative consciousness, felt its power and accepted the wisdom that comes through it, we will welcome a glorious rest afterwards.

My inner dialogue had created a disempowering story that I had lived by for over thirty years. I had allowed that story to hide my giftedness while I ran around compensating for what I believed to be defective about myself, until I was physically and mentally exhausted. The stories we tell ourselves are the stories that we live by and that disempowering tale about my daydreaming had became a handicap. Recognising my inner daydreamer as a precious gift has enabled me to embrace it and has brought me an enormous sense of freedom that allows me to open myself up to the creative muse.

I know that Mum's intentions were good. She wanted me to have a successful life and she believed that it came from doing practical things and doing them well. She was partly right. Without the discipline that she taught me, I wouldn't have the ability today to harness the creative energy that flows through me when I'm daydreaming, writing or at any other time. She was a teacher and was keen to develop all of my intellectual capabilities since she believed these were the keys to success and to having a good life. They certainly are valuable skills and so I'm eternally grateful to her for that.

I also know that now, from wherever she is, her message to me would be; 'Keep writing, be you. Do what feels true for you, use your gifts and have a wonderful life.' And then she would probably sign off, adding: 'P.S. I Love You!'

Discover your treasure:

1. What resonates with you about this story?
2. What disempowering story (or stories) about yourself has your inner dialogue created?
3. In what ways are you living by that story, or hiding it away and compensating for it, because you believe it to be true?
4. Where did the story come from – something that was said or an action that triggered your belief?
5. What true gifts or talents are hiding underneath each disempowering story?
6. How would your life be different if you were to embrace these talents and gifts and be grateful to the Universe for sending them your way?
7. What new story can you create to live by now?

26. HARNESSING THE INNER STORYTELLER

I get a warm, fuzzy feeling when I think about stories and cast my mind back to Aesop's Fables or Grimm's Fairy Tales and the plethora of other books I engaged with as a child. Although I'm not an avid reader of fiction, it's with awe I regard the work of modern authors such as J.K. Rowling in the genre of children's books and the raw and gritty works of Pulitzer-prizewinners such as Tennessee Williams, who wrote *A Streetcar Named Desire* (1947) and *Cat on a Hot Tin Roof* (1955) – creations that leave us on the edge of our seats. However, story is not always about curling up by the fireside with a cup of cocoa and a good read. It has, I have discovered, a sinister side too.

For many years, I wanted people to see me as a successful, intelligent, professional person who was infinitely capable and who had a perfect marriage, son, home and social life. I worried that people might judge me if they knew that I had spent most of my teenage years without my Mum, or that I'd had a dysfunctional relationship with food as a teenager, or that my son's birth was out of wedlock, or that I sometimes enjoyed daydreaming. Of course, I was projecting my own judgement of myself on to other people, believing that they would judge me in the same way that I criticised myself. However, it was also a reflection of the way that, as a society, we do tend to judge each other terribly. We take a few facts and craft a story around them and then make judgements about other people.

The other sinister element about storytelling is that we can build fear in our minds or the minds of others through the stories that we tell. We often see this sensationalising effect in the media, but it is a reflection of what we do in our conversations with ourselves and with others in our lives as well. We embellish facts to craft stories that eventually contain more speculation than truth. We have a word for narratives like these when they are about other people: we call them gossip. When they are fearful stories in the extreme, we call them paranoia. However, thinking the worst comes naturally to us – it's a survival mechanism and, as such, is hardwired into our psyche. When we are able to reflect upon what could happen or what something could mean, we have an opportunity to minimise the potential threat. However, all too often we simply have an overactive inner storyteller whose skills need to be honed and directed more positively.

Coming from an Irish family of great storytellers, I can tell you that an evening spent storytelling together can be a real blast. However, as I've always been aware that telling bleak stories is a family trait, I decided to take a personal inventory and see how I might have abused the gift of story myself and how I might have bought into the negative power of other people's gloomy tales.

What I discovered is that I have an Inner Storyteller who is always active, even when I'm in the world of dreams. However, I was embarrassed to realise that my Inner Storyteller can sometimes tell insidiously disempowering stories about work, health, money, people and the world in general, leaving me bewildered until I can become a witness to the story that I'm telling myself and recognise the imposter that is racing unchecked around my psyche. When our Inner Storyteller remains unharnessed, it can serve up a dish of fear, anxiety and gossip. But, with awareness, it can be unleashed into the service of serenity, love, health, prosperity and enchantment.

My Inner Storyteller has its roots in my childhood, where it authored a series of 'Things go Bump in the Night' and 'He Took my Toy' tales – and one fable in particular in which The Drama Queen was the central character. This particular story happened when I was seven years old. As a child, I had a vivid imagination which was a joy when it was focused on crafting an essay or playing a creative game, but which became a source of misery when it turned against me and brought demons and dragons into my life.

Lying in bed, staring at the ceiling, I toss and turn, unable to sleep. It is a dark, cold night and the wind is howling around our farmhouse, which has no trees or other houses nearby to protect it. I'm troubled because I can't find my favourite doll before bedtime. After playing with her outside earlier, I thought I had brought her inside with me but now I can't be certain.

'But what if you didn't?' says the voice of fear.

The voice of calm responds, 'I'm sure you did bring her in. She's probably warm and safe, hiding somewhere in the house.'

I relax briefly, before the voice of fear whispers, 'What if she's still out there, neglected and on her own?'

Calm says, 'I'm sure that she's just hiding and you'll find her inside in the morning.'

I settle briefly until the voice of fear ups the ante: 'You've left her outside and she's getting damaged by the wind and the rain.'

Calm, exasperated, says, 'Go to sleep and stop worrying – all will be well.'

Fear embellishes the story: 'There are cows out there and they might be trampling all over her – they might even eat her up.' An image flashes across my mind and I see my doll lying on the ground in the thin, purple and white dress that Granny made for her, soaked with rain and her face spattered with mud. A huge cow is ambling towards her, ready to stamp on her and eat her up. I'm now terrified.

Just when I can't take any more I hear footsteps outside my bedroom. 'Mum, Mum!' I shout. The door opens, the light is switched on and my Mum's head appears around the door.

'What's the matter? You should be asleep,' she says in a mildly irritated tone.

And then it all comes gushing out: 'My, my, my doll,' I blub, hardly able to speak, tears rolling down my cheeks. I don't need to be brave anymore so all the fretting comes bubbling out and my Mum sits on the bed. 'I'm not sure where my doll is – she might be outside in that rain and wind. I was playing with her and might have forgotten to bring her in. The cows might be eating her and if they get hold of her she'll be in t-t-tatters.' Only then do I pause for breath, which comes with a gulp.

'Well, cows don't eat dolls, they much prefer grass,' Mum assures me. 'It's very wet outside,' she says, pausing for a moment before getting up from the bed and leaving the room. Next, I hear my Dad's footsteps in his big boots going past my bedroom window outside. His padded anorak makes a familiar shushing sound as he moves.

The tension drains from my body and I relax for the first time in hours. I'm embraced by a warm tingle of safety, knowing that Dad has been assigned to a doll rescue mission. Blissfully, I hug my pillow thinking, 'Hurray – my doll is going to be saved from the hooves of the farm animals and the wicked wind and battering rain.'

Soon, Dad returns. As I hear his boots pace the floor downstairs, I sit up in bed and strain to hear the conversation he is having with my Mum. There's no doll out there, he's telling her. 'No doll outside – so she must be inside,' I reason to myself. 'Perhaps I did bring her in when we finished playing outside earlier?'

By this stage Granny has become involved and decides to search indoors for the doll. I'm calmer now that my mind has quieted from the earlier turmoil. The doll must be inside. Now I'm simply curious: 'Where can she have gone, she can't have just vanished into thin air?'

The voice of calm chimes in: 'Go to sleep and she'll probably turn up in the morning.'

As I'm drifting off to sleep, my Mum pokes her head around the door. 'Here's your doll,' she says, holding her up. The doll's not wet and in tatters. She's just as she was when I last saw her in her white and purple frock.

'Where was she?' I exclaim.

'Well! She was in the living room but she'd fallen behind a chair, so that's why you couldn't find her,' Mum explains.

Soon the doll is back in my arms. 'Thanks, Mum!' I say.

'Off to sleep now – night, night,' she replies, and with that she switches off the bedroom light, shuts the door and I snuggle up under the covers with my doll.

My doll was never lost, she was never in danger, she was never out in the cold, nor was she mauled by animals. She was there in the living room, waiting to be played with tomorrow. The demon thoughts have vanished. The monster cows stampeding across the field to trample upon her and eat her for a late night supper have disappeared. I can relax and allow myself to fall asleep.

The truth is that I could have relaxed anyway if I had refused to be seduced into the story that my imagination served up that night. As a small scared child with a vivid imagination on a cold, wet and windy, dark night, it was easy for me to get whisked down the rocky road that leads to disaster, but fortunately my parents were there to curb my drama. Today, that small scared child with her over-fertile imagination can still run the show, often insidiously, and it can take the best self-nurturing skills to calm her down.

We are all storytellers. The craft is as old as humankind. Since time immemorial, stories have been told in every genre – from cave paintings, legends and myths to modern literature. Stories have the power to educate, connect and bond, but also to distract, frighten and separate people. Stories are often based on grains of truth that are spiced up with condiments from the cupboards of our own wonderful imaginations. In the craft of literature, it is precisely these elements that are the fundamental ingredients of the trade and the basis of much of the magic. When we are detached observers who read a story as entertainment, it is a win–win situation for the author and the reader. However, when these ingredients are turned against us and other people in negative ways, they become harmful. When we turn the material of our own lives or those of others into melodramas, we can create anxiety and hurt.

According to Richard Bandler and John Grinder in their book, *The Structure of Magic*, it's in our nature to encode information in our minds by generalising, distorting and deleting the facts. That's how we create our version of the truth. We embellish information, turning the facts that we have gleaned into a story that may be quite different to that of another person who was witness to the same events. We draw conclusions about other people's intentions that may be complete conjecture.

Whether we spice up our tales with optimism, pessimism, shades of light and dark, humour, poignancy, fear, love, confidence, humility, shame, guilt, believing in people's positive or negative intentions, or a myriad of other elements – we must recognise that we're bringing our unique voice to everything we say. Mostly, we embellish facts with no awareness that we're story-crafting on the fly. If unchecked, our Inner Storyteller may habitually take us on a dizzying, emotional, rollercoaster ride, or into a dark cave. Our Inner Storyteller is a powerful resource that needs to be engaged wisely and mindfully.

The practice of meditation can connect us to our witnessing self so that, instead of buying into our own or other's emotional dramas, we can observe the storm and watch it go by. The temptation to chase after the tornados created by our own thoughts, or those of others, can be dangerously seductive. But this takes us away from our centre, making us less grounded in reality and more vulnerable to the wiles of our Inner Storyteller. It dampens down our energy and makes us more fearful, judgemental and more separate from other people. With a mindful approach, we can use our Inner Storyteller wisely to empower, inspire, connect and – ultimately – create a more peaceful and enchanting world.

Discover your treasure:

1. What resonates with you about this story?

2. Can you recognise any occasions when you might have turned the bare bones of fact into demon stories about yourself or other people?

3. What are the triggers that spark you into indulging in negative stories?

4. How do those stories make you think and feel about yourself or others and the world we live in?

5. Have you done reality checks to understand if other people have drawn the same conclusions as you have in a given circumstance?

6. What cultural or societal so called 'norms' might lie at the heart of your conclusions and those of others?

7. How would your life and your relationships be different if you committed to creating more compassionate and loving stories about yourself and others?

27. NATURAL SAGE

December 2010 was one of the coldest winters for many years. The ground was hard and packed with snow and ice as I drove carefully to the hospital to see David. Two nights earlier, I had taken David to hospital after he woke in the middle of the night, clammy and with severe stomach pains. It was the second time it had happened so we were less fearful on this occasion. Nevertheless, we were sure that the original diagnosis of 'gastritis or an ulcer' that the consultant had given wasn't accurate. At the hospital, they ran a battery of tests and discovered that gallstones and an inflamed gallbladder were in fact the source of the pain. The consultant was ready to remove David's gallbladder in an emergency procedure on December 4th.

This was the very same day that we had arranged to collect Sage, our new puppy, from the breeder. As I crawled the car along the slippery roads I wondered, 'How am I going to collect a puppy by myself? I can't have a puppy bouncing around in the car – I need some help!' The only time I'd ever even held a puppy was the day we chose Sage. David, in contrast, had grown up with dogs and now he was facing surgery and a convalescence period just as we were about to experience the joys and tribulations of owning an eight week old puppy.

Upon my arrival at the hospital, I found David sitting on the edge of his bed fully clothed, shoe laces tied, ready to go. 'So, what's happening?' I asked.

'The pain's gone and I've told the consultant that I'm not having surgery today,' David explained, adding, 'besides which, the consultant said that was fine and he could remove my gallbladder later as elective surgery. So today, I want to go and get Sage.'

So we set out for the breeder's house, stopping briefly at home to collect a box, vet bedding and the cuddly toy that I had bought for our new puppy. When the breeder invited us into her dining room to complete the paperwork, we could hear the scratchy barking of the puppies in the next room and the deep tones of their Mum as she detected a threat to her litter. The paperwork seemed to take forever to complete, after which the breeder went to get Sage. Soon she emerged with him in her arms and gently placed him in mine. He was shaking with fear and I felt cruel for taking him away from all he had ever known. If he knew how well we planned to take care of him, he'd be happy, I thought. We said our goodbyes to the breeder and went to the car.

As soon as I placed Sage on the back seat, he climbed on to his bedding and nuzzled up to the cuddly toy that I had bought for him. As David drove away, Sage continued to shake even as I tried to soothe him with calming words.

By the time we arrived home, Sage had been sick from the motion of the car combined with his fear. We had set up a dog crate for him in the kitchen, where we hoped he'd feel safe. He scrambled inside and then stood looking out at us. Although the door was open, he refused to come out for a while and then he hopped onto the kitchen floor, quickly turned around and went back inside the crate again. David and I watched, fascinated by the antics of this gorgeous little creature. Eventually food enticed Sage to stay out of his crate for longer. By ten o'clock in the evening he decided that it was time for bed and he went to sleep in his crate, only waking at 6 o'clock the following morning to empty his bladder.

Soon Sage's confidence grew and he was roaming around the kitchen and then into the hallway and eventually he braved the stairs. For several weeks, his main activities were sleeping, eating and emptying his bladder – up to twenty times a day. David took charge of managing toilet training and kept a list documenting how often Sage managed to 'go' outside versus having an accident inside. We also took Sage to puppy-training classes, but he was more interested in playing with the other puppies than doing what the trainer wanted him to do.

As Sage grew older and bolder, he became ready to venture outside, although it took time to build his confidence and to persuade him to go any distance from the house. Initially, he'd walk comfortably for a few metres and then turn back, whining and pulling on the lead to go home. The site of a plastic bag waving in the breeze was enough to terrify him.

Sage grew rapidly and was soon ready for longer walks that opened up his world and ours. We'd been living in our neighbourhood for ten years and realised that we barely knew many of our neighbours until we began walking Sage. Other dog walkers stopped to let their dogs and children say hello to Sage. 'Have you just moved into the neighbourhood?' several asked us.

Besides introducing us to new people, Sage opened us up to the beauty of nature as we discovered new and interesting places to walk him. One of those was a glorious six-mile walk that we did in the company of friends, following a map that had us traversing the Oxfordshire countryside. We walked by an old railway line, through fields, across roads, down by paddocks, and on and on as we engaged in abundant chatter and laughter. We halted occasionally as Sage negotiated the stiles. Sometimes he found a gap in the fence to get through, whereas at other times he stood rooted to the ground like an obstinate child until he was lifted over the stile. Then he'd scamper on again.

The wind was bracing and my ears stung as it whistled past. If only I had remembered to wear the white woolly hat that David had given me as a stocking filler at Christmas! Thinking about whistling winds and woolly hats, I couldn't help but remember my childhood in Ireland and a family holiday at the seaside one July. While we'd normally expect to be sporting bikinis on holiday, the extreme weather that summer meant that my Mum bought me a soft woolly hat in rusty brown and cobalt blue.

We were staying in a picturesque holiday fishing village called Mullaghmore, on the northwest Atlantic coast in County Sligo. The village sits close to the rugged Atlantic Ocean in the lap of a monolithic mountain known as Ben Bulben. In Gaelic, *An Mullach Mór* means great summit, which refers to the infamous crest of Ben Bulben visible against the distant horizon. Today, Mullaghmore is a surfers' paradise, with relentless crashing waves that are a testament to the might of the vigorous Atlantic Ocean. However, in the 1970s, it wasn't a typical holiday resort for children. It was unspoilt with none of the commercial entertainment attractions that we adored as kids. This was to be a different kind of holiday, an immersion in nature, an opportunity to experience the sheer magnificence of the Almighty – and, although I couldn't have articulated it that way at the time, my memories of it were exactly like that.

The weather was inclement, windy with squally showers that are typical of the northwest Atlantic coast. Summer colds weren't uncommon and on this holiday my siblings and I came down with sneezing, runny noses, sore throats and elevated temperatures after only a few days. Mum went shopping in the local town of Bundoran in the neighbouring county to buy us medicine and woolly hats – which you might imagine would be hard to come by in July, but no, not there: they had a wonderful selection, fortunately. I can still feel the soft wool of mine in my hands.

Being in County Sligo, another feature of our holiday was that we were close to my Mum's sister, Auntie Nancy, who later came to look after us around the time we lost Mum. Nancy was a nun and lived in the grand, old convent building in Sligo that belonged to the Sisters of Mercy. Like many of the Sisters of Mercy, she was a teacher, her subject being science. She was passionate about both science and nature.

While she was studying for her science degree, Nancy worked on a particular project: she collected one hundred species of wild plants. She kept them in a photograph album, which she would sometimes bring out to show us and to which she continued to add new specimens. I was always impressed by how beautiful and neat it looked. She explained that she had to pick the plants, identify their Latin names and their everyday names, and then press them between sheets of paper under heavy books until they were dried. She carefully placed them in her album with elaborately hand written labels bearing their names.

I was in the car on several occasions while my Mum drove and Nancy sat in the passenger seat, when Nancy's eagle eye would spot a new species that hadn't yet made it into the pages of her plant album. As soon as she'd pointed out the precious plant that had grabbed her attention, Mum would pull over, stop the car and out they would get to snip a cutting from the latest discovery. Keen nature lovers, they were as excited as each other to find these wonderful plants growing wild and free along the roadside.

And so our holiday in Mullaghmore was touched by this love of nature too. Nancy introduced us to a three-mile walk around Mullaghmore Head, much of it along the Atlantic coast. Every day, we'd set off at about five o'clock in the evening to make our way around the Head. It was nature at its most awesome with great crashing waves, bracing winds and a breathtakingly stunning landscape for miles, reaching towards the craggy summit of Ben Bulben in the distance. It was a fast walk too – too cold to saunter – and invigorating, with the force of life pulsating through us and the sights, sounds and smells of nature delightfully intoxicating every sense. It was a rich experience filled with chattering and giggling, before the sheer beauty of the landscape combined with the effort of our walk literally took our breath away.

On these walks, Nature gave us a grand display of the abundance of the Almighty, a great show in which the orchestra was directed to give it everything – violin, cello, double bass, brass, wind, drums and cymbals giving it their all to reach the crescendo, that note where you lose yourself and become one with nature. Indeed, it is easy to understand how County Sligo was such an inspiration for the poet W.B. Yeats, whose most famous works include 'The Lake Isle of Innisfree', in which he romanticises his childhood memories of living on the northwest coast of Ireland.

Back in Oxfordshire in 2011, our little party of walkers had reached another stile and so I was flipped out of my daydream. Our walk took place in countryside very different to the northwest Atlantic coast but was nevertheless beautiful. Three miles into our walk, an astonishing sight graced our eyes when a small herd of fallow deer galloped elegantly across the landscape in front of us. It was an amazing sight, such as you only ever expect to see in nature films. And yet there it was right before us – five or six deer gliding across the landscape. Another four joined the delightful dance and then three more followed. It looked like Dasher, Dancer, Prancer, Vixen, Comet and Cupid had decided to take a well-earned rest after Christmas, in the Oxfordshire fields.

The herd of deer grew smaller and smaller, until the animals were barely visible in the distance. We walked on and on before arriving at a welcoming English village pub. As we sat in the beer garden and enjoyed our drinks I realised how inspiring, energising and invigorating it is to walk in nature – such wonderful exercise and entertainment and completely free.

Waking in nature has always been a great pleasure of mine, perhaps inspired by those walks around Mullaghmore Head on summer evenings in the 1970s. Because of Sage, I rediscovered that the joy of nature is a gift. Many of our passions, I believe, have their roots in our childhoods and reconnecting with those experiences that brought us joy can be a wonderful way to reignite our zest for life.

When I reflect on how the situation with David's health created a dilemma for us because we had been planning to collect Sage the same day that he was scheduled to have his operation, I can see now that it might have been a case of perfect timing. In this particular instance – and every situation is unique, with its own medical circumstances, so what was right for us certainly wouldn't be the case for everyone else – delaying the operation gave us the time to consult with a variety of people and to research into finding an integrated approach to managing his gallstones that would resonate with him, as well as with his medical consultant.

We are human beings and are part of nature's beauty too. It is easy to forget that, when the convenience lifestyle beckons. We can be seduced by quick fixes rather than taking the time to discover what is right for us – sometimes we have to make quick decisions in life but often we can take our time. The closer to nature that we can live, the more aligned we are with our essential nature as human beings. That doesn't mean that we have to become reclusive and live self-sufficiently in the middle of nowhere. We can take a few steps back from the hustle and bustle of our world and tune into our own nature on a daily basis. That might be by walking in nature, meditating, painting or in any way that unplugs us from being constantly switched on and revved-up. Our bodies, minds and souls all need that if we *are to become* our optimal selves.

Discover your treasure:

1. What resonates with you about this story?
2. What does 'living a life that is more in tune with nature mean to you?'
3. How have you incorporated nature's gifts into the life script that you are creating for yourself?
4. How well do you nourish yourself with natural healthy foods, tuning into your body's wisdom and giving your body the rest and exercise it needs?
5. Do you recognize that you have a true nature and that when you live in alignment with your nature life gets easier?
6. Do you recognize the tension that is created in your life when you're not living in a way that is aligned with your true nature?
7. What changes do you need to build a life script that is more aligned with your natural self – that feels right for you?

28. ROCKING THE BOAT

As I was nearing the end of writing this book, an unexpected hurdle presented itself. When I reviewed the book, I realised that one of the greatest challenges in writing a memoir was that it meant 'rocking the boat' and writing about things that other people might prefer I didn't mention.

That is why I had set my intention at the outset to write a wisdom memoir. It was not meant to be an opportunity to trot out salacious tales about either myself or others. Instead, my intention was to share stories about my life as I had experienced them through the filter of the age I was when each event occurred; and then to reflect upon those stories with the wisdom that I have now. It entailed selecting carefully what material to share so that the story would be authentic and meaningful, while limiting recollections that might cause embarrassment or hurt to the people concerned. That made for a tricky balance to strike.

Life has been challenging for me at times, as it is for everyone and those challenges were often made more bearable or more difficult by the behaviour of other people. Hence my dilemma about how to tackle the thorny problem of telling it the way it was, even if some people wouldn't necessarily want to hear how it was for me. While it was relatively easy to share specific facts, because those couldn't be refuted, my truth about what happened was determined by my personal experience – the window through which I saw events and which was framed by my beliefs, values and identity – while other people might have had a different perspective on events, because it was shaped by theirs.

The problem took me back to my childhood growing up in a big family in Ireland. Like many others, my Irish Catholic family thought it important to keep up appearances and uphold the myth of the perfect family. We went to the right schools, wore the right clothes and were encouraged to speak properly. Yet there was no place in the household for conversations that were real, that acknowledged feelings or created a space in which everyone's voice could be heard.

There was little time for rocking the boat. 'You're so difficult – why can't you be like any other little girl?' my Mum would tell me. She meant: 'Be nice, sweet and show love all the time and don't make waves.' Don't question things – just do what you're told as it's much more convenient for everybody. Don't express feelings that are not wholeheartedly positive – it's inconvenient.

With five children and two working parents in the household, there was limited time for individual views and opinions – everyone had to go with the flow. As a youngster, I was dressed in exactly the same way as my elder sister and, like most families, we all ate the same foods. We learned piano because that seemed to be the thing to do. On the odd occasion when there was any discussion, it seemed to take place between my parents or sometimes with my elder sister, Mary, as if she could speak for all the children. This wasn't something that was unique to my family – fitting in was the way that most big households survived.

As a sensitive child with thoughts and opinions of my own, who abhorred being herded, I wanted the opportunity to speak for myself; and when I didn't have this I felt frustrated. These feelings therefore often came out as a tantrum when I'd reached the end of my tether.

I grew up believing that I was 'difficult' and that being emphatic was the only way to get my voice heard. At the same time, I struggled with the guilt I felt if I rocked the boat by saying something that went contrary to popular opinion. In time, I learned to compensate for my 'difficult' self by trying to be nice. But this behaviour felt weak and inauthentic to me too, because – while it achieved my goal of being liked – it wasn't an effective way to be heard. Being nice is often a form of passive, withdrawn compliance and lacks power. And so, I oscillated between feeling guilty that I might be regarded as being difficult and feeling the impotence that comes with being passively nice.

What I wanted instead was to be effective while respecting other people; and that, I realised, comes from recognising that there is no such thing as a neutral stance – either we are colluding with the status quo or we're advocating for something different.

When we turn a blind eye or say 'it's got nothing to do with me', we're abdicating our power. If we do not agree with something and yet we remain quiet, we're effectively saying yes to it and we're being untrue to ourselves. We might find that circumstances make it difficult or even socially inappropriate for us to make a stand – such as when someone is lecturing us from the stage at a conference. Often, however, that isn't the case: we simply choose to be quiet and then complain afterwards. But it's worth remembering that we may be depriving our friends, families, work colleagues, customers or companies of the benefit of our wisdom.

On the other hand, it's not appropriate to beat everyone up with our opinions either. Dominating conversations, throwing tantrums, emotionally blackmailing people, thoughtlessly firing out messages via social media that may be hurtful or intimidating for other people – these are not enlightened ways to be. While most of us don't do these things in the extreme, it is worth asking ourselves whether we ever dominate conversations and try to sell our opinions to other people without giving them the space in which to express their own views.

We are not powerless - in fact we are infinitely powerful and we have a responsibility to use our power wisely. We are called to rock the boat when the boat needs rocking – otherwise why would we have strong feelings about things? At the same time, we have to be mindful of how we use our power – if we are not careful, we can become tyrants, constantly making waves and wanting our own way for the sake of it. We can feel justified in making our voice heard, with little regard to the ways that it can destroy relationships and throw individuals and groups into conflict and disarray. Well, we might have got our own way but at what price? When this happens, we are acting from our egos and that does not lead to authentic power with integrity.

When we're either competitively bashing people with our opinions, or remaining withdrawn and refusing to give our gifts at all, our communication is not coming from a place of heart and soul. In organisations, the more aggressive approach often results in having an idea carried through, but it might not be the best solution and not everyone will agree with it. However, when we assert ourselves with integrity, we're coming from our hearts rather than our egos. We bring positive energy into our communications and show respect for individuals, yet without hiding, glossing over or whitewashing issues to avoid rocking the boat.

At times, we might deliberately choose to rock the boat in order to be effective. When we combine our Inner Warrior energy with our hearts, we can rock the boat with integrity and respect for others in order to create change and explore new shores. Discovering a way to express my voice authentically and yet mindfully has been one of the challenges that I have had to overcome on the journey to creating this wisdom memoir. I wish you the courage, confidence and compassion to express your authentic voice too.

Discover your treasure:
1. What resonates with you about this story?
2. What stories do you tell yourself about expectations you believe that other people have of you, for example;
   a. to be nice, charming or silent rather than honest
   b. or to hammer home your point so that you don't lose face, even if you're not sure that you believe it yourself?
3. What stories do you tell yourself about how you actually behave – for example too nice, too aggressive or something else?
4. What story do you tell yourself about what would happen if you were to express your voice in a way that feels real?
5. Think about a time when you felt good about communicating your message – how did you achieve that?
6. Think about a time when you didn't feel good about your communication – what got in the way?
7. How can you express yourself authentically with courage, confidence and compassion?

29. CELEBRATING SUCCESSES

S itting across the breakfast table from Ryan, I asked, 'When is your graduation ceremony?' I was expecting it to take place several months after he had completed his degree in May.

'July,' he said.

'What date in July?' I asked.

'Middle,' came his reply.

'That's when I'm going to be on a course in Santa Cruz!' I said, as if that was going to make the university reconsider its graduation date. 'Are you sure?' I asked.

'Well, that's when it was last year,' he responded.

'Oh dear,' I thought, 'that's tricky.'

Reading my mind, he said, 'Don't worry about it, just go on your course.'

For four years, beginning with a foundation year followed by his three-year degree course, I'd been looking forward to watching Ryan graduate and I wanted to be there. At the same time, I was really looking forward to going to Santa Cruz for three weeks on an inspiring course with world-class trainers, where I would meet an exciting group of students. My NLP mind said, 'Claire, you have a values conflict going on and you're going to have to choose.'

I already knew the answer. Being there with Ryan at his graduation and celebrating his success afterwards were paramount. So I told him, 'I'm coming to your graduation whatever date it falls on. I want to be there.'

As I recalled the times in the past when I had been torn between spending time with Ryan and fulfilling my work commitments, I often regretted the choice I'd made to work when it could have waited. Drifting back through my memories, I recalled an occasion when I promised Ryan that I'd watch him sing Christmas songs with his nursery class.

The carol service was at noon, which meant that I would need to take a two-hour lunch break. However, considering I often left work so late that I was switching out the lights as I walked out the door, that shouldn't have been a problem. I spoke to my boss, who agreed I could take the long lunch, but not before remarking that he'd usually have expected me to take the afternoon off as holiday. I escaped work just in time and made my way to the hall.

As I walked in, the children were arranged in a choir to sing their songs. When I took a seat in the front row next to other parents, I spotted Ryan in the group at almost exactly the same time as he clocked me. He instantly became animated and, turning towards the children on each side, he said, 'There's my Mummy, look, there's my Mummy!' Smiling, I waved to him and he waved back as the children prepared to sing. With a joyful heart, I realised the importance of showing up to see and hear him that day.

Back in the present, I pondered the concept of acknowledging successes and realised that I had never taken the time to acknowledge anything that I had ever achieved myself before striving for the next step. It wasn't something that people did back in the 1970s and 1980s in Ireland – doing well was expected of us. I remember my first report from secondary school when, as a newbie, I got four grade As and several grade Bs. My Italian grade was poor and my Mum focused on that. What had happened with the Italian? Why wasn't it better? I pointed to the other grades and she simply said, 'Keep that up.' So the ground rules were set for my self-talk around achievement.

Watching the way we live as a society, I suspect that many people have had a similar experience and not celebrated the successes in their lives. Instead, we carry on racing from one thing to the next, hardly stopping to draw breath. Our striving is relentless, affording little space for celebration. That's probably why I and many other parents gush so effusively about our children's achievements today.

The Hindu Bhagavad Gita calls on us to reap our harvest and feed from it before starting the cycle again: activity followed by rest, knowledge gained followed by knowledge used. But we westerners don't like to let the grass grow under our feet or to be caught napping. We're terrified that if we don't keep running we'll end up watching the world whooshing by us.

Ryan's graduation day arrives and we're up early to get to Royal Festival Hall on the South Bank in London. We're seated in the hall with the orchestra playing in the background. Then the show begins. News reporter Jon Snow is awarded an honorary doctorate for services to journalism. He stands to give a short speech. After reminding us that it is Nelson Mandela's ninety-fifth birthday, he goes on to tell us what it was like to wait outside the prison in South Africa where Mandela was about to be released after his twenty-seven year incarceration. He explains how he had with him an old photograph of Mandela, showing him as a man twenty-seven years younger, and his fear was that he wouldn't recognise the now much older Mandela as he emerged from prison. However, as soon as he appeared, Jon Snow tells us that Mandela's aura was unmistakable. No photograph was needed to recognise him immediately.

I'm moved to tears. Today is a celebration of Jon Snow's honorary doctorate, Nelson Mandela's birthday and Ryan's graduation from university. 'Wow,' I think, 'Ryan's in good company, celebrating on this day.'

The Dean reminds everyone that the creative path is not always easy, but that it is often those people who think in different ways to most folk who become the individuals who change the world. He reminds us that the university has alumni such as art director and typographer Neville Brodie, who has worked on magazines such as *The Face* and *Arena*, as well a range of music album covers, and who is the founder of his own design practice. Brodie's tendency to break the mould was frowned upon back in the 1970s by his university lecturers. However, thankfully the world has changed.

Ryan is at the beginning of his career, with every opportunity to shape the future. And the occasion reminds me that, every day, we all stand at the edge of the chance to make changes in our world. We can embrace this opportunity or stand back from it. The truth is that until we acknowledge ourselves and recognise our own worth, we can't expect anyone else to do so either. And, once we do, we will have less need to collect certificates.

So what stops us from showing up in our own authentic way in the world? What prevents us from bringing our gifts and creating positive change along the way? In exploring that question, I've come to realise that fear lies at the root. Fear of failure: looking foolish; wasting our time and our money; or even making ourselves destitute. Ironically, we can also fear success: becoming overwhelmed by the task and the expectations of others; becoming too visible and being talked about; being chastised or attacked for our views. But when we truly acknowledge our own voice and recognise our gifts, we can get beyond that fear.

Then I ask myself, what would our world be like if people such as Nelson Mandela, Mother Teresa, Albert Einstein, Rosa Parks, Steve Jobs, and others of their ilk had allowed themselves to be held back by fear of failure or fear of success? It seems as if these people have been empowered by the Universe to make a difference. They – and indeed we all – have been empowered by the Universe to take up our place and make our actions count.

Now I ask myself, 'How would I live if I truly acknowledged the unique gifts that I can bring and believed that I was empowered by the Universe? How would I think differently about my purpose in life? How would I think about the value I can give to other people?' It takes me way beyond the boxes within which I learned to operate through my experiences of education and the corporate world. These are often places where thinking differently is encouraged but with the massive constraints of being in an environment that is highly logical, analytical and relatively controlled in contrast to the creative freedom that thinking differently requires.

It strikes me that celebrating our achievements and successes is fundamental to recognising that we are empowered by the Universe. This in turn gives us the courage we need to speak with our true voices and have real conversations with others. It is not a privilege to be able to share ourselves with the world: it is the reason that we are here on earth at this time in history. Celebrating our successes is central to owning who we are, recognising our gifts and filling ourselves with the courage to let our voices be heard.

So let's finish this story with applause for all of our successes – and let this mark the beginning of a journey back in time during which we begin to identify those stories where we know that we did our best, yet where we brushed success off with a dismissive shrug. It's time now to acknowledge ourselves with words that feel appropriate, such as: 'that was wonderful' or 'I did great, especially under those circumstances', or 'I totally aced it', or 'that was tricky, and I learned such a lot'.

We can celebrate through what author Sarah Ban Breathnach calls 'simple abundance'. It might be a gift, or a trip to a special place, or eating at a favourite restaurant, or just taking some time out to acknowledge and appreciate ourselves – and most of all to mark our achievements. And that's what we did at Ryan's graduation – we turned it into a wonderful day of celebration doing whatever *he* wanted to do on his special day and we captured all the joyful moments on camera.

Whatever you do, celebrate! Nothing is complete until what you have accomplished is acknowledged and integrated – and that is what the ritual of celebration is all about.

Discover your treasure:

1. What resonates with you about this story?
2. How good are you at celebrating your success stories?
3. What messages did you get as a child and as a young adult about achieving things?
4. Do you adequately acknowledge your success before striving to plant new seeds?
5. When you don't acknowledge your successes or even mark the completion of something, what stops you?

6. How do you feel when you stop to integrate what you have achieved, rather than shrugging it off?

7. Consider how celebrating might boost your vibration and energise you for the next chapter in your life story.

30. A LIFE REWRITTEN

On a recent trip to Ireland for a family get-together, I was uncertain about how my book of life stories, would be received by my family, since many of my tales featured them too. I sat with my four siblings and our father around a brightly burning fire-pit in Mary's garden under a starry August sky, while we talked about old times. Much of our storytelling around the fire-pit that night was sparked by the fact that my siblings had been reading a draft manuscript of *The Tao of Storytelling*. Their memories and stories mostly contain the same facts as mine, but often their experiences were different, reminding me that to each of us our story is true from our own perspective. For us, it was a rare chance to reminisce together, since these days only Mary, Tom and our father live in Ireland. William – whom we now call Bill – lives in Spain and Edel in Australia, while I live in the UK. For our respective partners, it was an opportunity to hear some of our stories about growing up in Ireland together and to share some of their tales with us too. And, for our children, it was a chance to tap into their family history.

Even small children want to understand the people who came before them. Edel's daughter Amelie, although only four years old, was curious about why her Granny (our Mum) was not there and so she asked Edel 'Where is my Granny?'

'She lives with the Angels,' Edel explained, 'and so she's always with us.' That story works for Amelie and it resonates with us too as Mum still lives in our minds and in our hearts.

Like clockwork, before the night was through my father reminded me of the plaque my Mum had bought me when I was twelve – the one that said: 'How beautiful it is to do nothing and then rest afterwards.' Thankfully my story about that plaque has been transformed and so I was simply amused to hear about it again.

The stories that we tell about our lives are the stories that we live by. We are all storytellers – the scriptwriters, film directors and moviemakers of our own lives. Whatever the facts, we choose the meaning. If we don't like the meaning, we can re-edit our story – writing and rewriting not just to shape our future but our present and our history as well – until we have created a rich tapestry that resonates with who we are now.

The Tao of Storytelling began as a search for enchantment somewhere out there. It was an inspired journey that

I embarked upon with no idea of where it would lead. As I first wrote down some of these stories in a blog, I discovered that there was wisdom to be gleaned from each vignette. That is when I decided to write this book as a wisdom memoir.

It was an unfolding journey whose course I couldn't have predicted before I began. The early days stories were easy. Like every other child, when I was small I didn't think about who I was or examine why I did something. I knew that I loved dolls, Lego, Fuzzy Felt and jigsaws. Cakes, mashed potato and pear dessert had me drooling. Anything that was shiny, glittery or pink attracted me like a magpie. Then, as I discovered reading, I became a big fan of fairy stories and characters such as Noddy and Big Ears and Topsy and Tim, until I progressed to Enid Blyton's books about the antics of those girls in mythical boarding schools. Writing essays at school filled me with excitement. In my simple child's mind, I had no concept of myself as having an id, an ego and a super ego as Freud defined them. I thought what I thought and wasn't aware of having a self that had an opinion about myself, or an opinion about my opinion.

That all changed when I was thrown into the introspective dark place that came with the loss of my Mum. When I got to the darker stories, in my writing, there was no enchantment, no light – just a sense of gratitude that those days were behind me now and that I have gone on to create a happy life for myself. The dark days created an impasse in my writing. I couldn't skip over my teenage years and bounce from childish innocence to adulthood: there would have been an obvious gap in the book.

After I'd completed my training in storytelling as a performing art, I resumed writing the book and was ready to confront the difficult stories. Even though I'd believed that those stories were behind me – as I explored them further, I had to accept that I was still burdened by them. And I was ashamed to admit that I felt slightly victimized by them.

Excavating further, I was able to let go of that theme and realise that I had never been a victim and that instead I had been on my own healing journey. I came to regard my stories as priceless gems. Sifting through the details, I relegated those that didn't serve me while paying more attention to those that energised me, because they had a ring of truth about them. This made for a more enchanting story to live by, a more empowering springboard for the future. I realised the infinite power that I and everyone else has to choose the meanings we attach to events. We write our stories as human beings by sieving through the information that is available to us. We experience much of life subconsciously, while on autopilot, and we believe the output, whether it's good, bad or ugly. But we can choose to bring our experiences into our conscious awareness and thereby write more empowering narratives about them.

The miracle for me was that, in excavating that cave within, I came upon chinks of light. As I moved towards them they opened up and there was treasure. As I followed the light within these dark stories, new narratives emerged that had brighter, lighter and more playful energy. Within each of the stories there was enchantment that came from the recognition of who I was then, of the people who had been beacons of light on my journey, and greater understanding of the people who I had perceived as the villains.

When it is dark enough you can see the stars.

Ralph Waldo Emerson

The most profound discovery was the effect that re-scripting these stories has had on me. Instead of being a burden that I had to carry, they were transformed in a rich history of enchanted moments. There was gratitude towards people who had shown extraordinary kindness, love and generosity and who had been empowering teachers and mentors – and, of course, moments of forgiveness, which takes time and is a healing art.

I was transformed in turn. I had rewritten my own history, authentically, based on the same facts but attaching to them more empowering meanings. I brought people that I had thought were gone, back into my life through these stories and built rich connections with them through the memories that I patched together. It made me a more confident, lighter, more open, relaxed and loving person.

Other people said that the stories touched them by resonating with them in either a personal way or by hinting at a universal truth. After I had written the first draft of the book and told people about how personally transformative it was to write these stories, I found people talking to me about Narrative Therapy and Narrative Mediation. Keen to find out more, I discovered the work of Michael White in Australia on Narrative Therapy. In his book *Maps of Narrative Practice*, he talks about the idea that our identities are created not in isolation but in relationship to the other people in our lives.

When important relationships in our lives are broken or difficult, it affects how we feel about ourselves. That, in turn, determines the stories that we tell and the stories that we live by. The challenging tales tend to be the ones that offer the greatest opportunity for healing, so it's essential that we don't gloss over these in a Pollyanna fashion. There is richness for all parties concerned within these stories, but it is not our job to demand that other people acknowledge their misdemeanours – although it's wonderful when they do. It is our job to clear our side of the street – own our part in any story – and to forgive ourselves for our wrongdoings as well as forgiving others when we are ready to do so.

Author Michael White talks about re-membering (bringing together the significant people who have contributed to our lives and to whose lives we have also contributed in our own personal narratives). He also talks about re-authoring lives –and by that he means finding alternative narratives to our problem stories and rewriting them in a more empowering way.

The re-membering and re-authoring of my own life is what I have done in this book, and that is why the experience of writing it was so transformational. It led me to training in storytelling and narrative practice and co-founding The Story Mill to bring this transformational work to organisations, teams and individuals, enabling people to create empowering narratives with which to communicate both inside and outside their organisations.

The discovery that stories provide the scripts that we live by, highlighted the importance of changing old scripts that don't serve us. When we carry these sorts of scripts around in our subconscious they create a drain on our energy, but we can heal them and use them to build a springboard to an empowering future. In the process, we get to rewrite the past and to acknowledge our dreams, values, beliefs and the personal gifts that we want to take with us on the next steps of our journey.

I hope that you are inspired to remember and rescript your own stories so that you can discover the treasure in your own life and build an empowering future for yourself.

I encourage you to excavate your 'once upon a times' and discover your own 'happy ever afters', so that your life becomes richer, more connected and more enchanting than you could ever have dreamt possible. And remember that the stories you tell yourself are the stories that you live by – so be sure to create stories that empower you.

Discover your treasure:
1. What resonates with you about this story?
2. Now that you have read the book, which story themes resonate most with you?

3. In what ways do they resonate?

4. Take each story theme and write about areas of your life where you identify with them.

5. Use the exercises related to each theme to help you discover your own wisdom.

6. Having discovered your wisdom, how can you rescript your stories in a way that opens your heart and reclaims your power?

7. How can you also write the kind of life script that you want to shape your future. Go ahead and do it now.

FURTHER READING

Celica Ahern, *P.S. I Love You* (HarperCollins, 2012)

Richard Bandler and John Grinder, *The Structure of Magic* (Science and Behavior Books, 1989)

Eric Bearne, *Games People Play* (Penguin, 2010)

Sean Covey, *The Seven Habits of Highly Effective Teens* (Simon & Schuster, 2004)

Roberts Dilts and Stephen Gilligan, *The Hero's Journey* (Crown House, 2009)

Masaru Emoto, *The Hidden Messages in Water* (Pocket Books, 2005)

Viktor E. Frankl, *Man's Search for Meaning* (Rider Books, 2004)

Malcolm Gladwell, *Outliers* (Penguin, 2009)

Séamus Ó Néill, Dánta do pháistí (*Poems for Children*), Sáirséal agus Dill 1949 - (Cló Iar-Chonnacht)

Steven Pressfield, *The Legend of Bagger Vance* (Bantam Books, 2001)

Ramsden A & Hollingsworth S, The Storyteller's Way (Hawthorn Press, 2013)

Chuck Spezzano, *30 Days to Find Your Perfect Mate* (Vermilion, 1994)

Michael White, *Maps of Narrative Practice* (W.W. Norton & Co, 2007)

Nick Williams, *The Work We Were Born to Do* (Balloon View, 2010)